FLY FISHING PLAYBOOK

2nd edition

Duane Redford

HEADWATER
BOOKS

STACKPOLE
BOOKS

0 11557 01543 0

This book is dedicated to all of the great guides
I've had the opportunity to work with, my family and friends,
and most importantly, Allie, Parker, and my wife, Janet,
who has always been there to pick up the slack as I continue
to chase my passion for fish on the fly rod.

Published by
STACKPOLE BOOKS
5067 Ritter Road
Mechanicsburg, PA 17055
www.stackpolebooks.com

Printed in the United States of America

10 9 8 7 6 5 4 3 2 1

Second edition

Cover design by Caroline Stover
Cover image by the author
Photos by the author
Illustrations by Dave Hall

Library of Congress Cataloging-in-Publication Data

Redford, Duane, author.
  Fly fisher's playbook / Duane Redford. — 2nd edition.
     pages cm
  Includes bibliographical references and index.
  ISBN 978-0-8117-1543-0 (alk. paper)
  1. Nymph fishing. 2. Fly fishing. I. Title.
  SH456.15.R43 2015
  799.12'4—dc23
                                        2014039055

Contents

Introduction

"No man ever steps in the same river twice,
for it's not the same river and he's not the same man."
—*Heraclitus*

That quote really speaks to me. Maybe it's a function of where I spend most of my days on the river, or maybe it's a testament to how long I've been slinging a fly rod. Not sure. I do know this: each time I go out to the river, I learn something, and the river I fly-fish changes each time, too.

I spend most of my fly-fishing and guiding days on the famous South Platte River, near Deckers, Colorado, a legendary tailwater that is known for healthy, strong fish and technical drifts. I cut my teeth guiding on this river through high and low water, heavy recreational pressure, and forest fires. It's been a great ride, and I am a better angler because of it.

As a former coach, I learned long ago to give your opponent credit where it is due, but I also learned that every opponent has weaknesses. In order to exploit your opponent's weaknesses, you must be able to define your own. In other words, one must play to his own strengths while minimizing weaknesses to compete and win. I approach the river the same way.

Years ago, I began to document each day on the river. I carried a small journal and a pen tucked into my fly vest. I wrote down everything from water flows and clarity, to weather conditions, hatches, and flies used. After roughly five years of diligent record keeping, I began to see trends within the journal database—not only obvious trends, but clear patterns. I could easily see my weaknesses as a fly fisher.

I try to approach the river in the same manner a quarterback approaches the line of scrimmage. A play has been called in the huddle, but it's likely to change depending on how the defense lines up. Just like a quarterback, you have to be able to "audible" or change the play on the fly. You have to be able to overcome the defense with a solid, quick decision. Simply put, you have a base play called, but because of conditions, you need to change the play.

Trout have several defenses, both physically and conditionally. In other words, they have defenses gained from how they're built and where they live. They gain substantial defenses from their surroundings. Clearly, you'll have to make changes, as a quarterback does, when you get a look at the presented defense—changes that make sense, changes that follow a system.

Whereas I used to guess what the next move should be, now I decide on the next best option to overcome present conditions. Without guessing, I could stay on the offensive, keeping the pressure on the fish. A systematic approach to nymphing becomes readily apparent. The focus became cycling through options to ensure technique and riggings were exactly what the conditions called for. Instead of willing fish to eat, I began to force or coerce fish to eat. The systematic approach changed my way of fishing.

The *Fly Fisher's Playbook* was born. Similar to a football playbook that each player must memorize, the *Fly Fisher's Playbook* outlines basic plays designed to effectively work against presented defenses or fishing conditions. It shows the importance of each component and skill, and how each component relies on the next. The *Fly Fisher's Playbook* not only has basic plays like nymph rigging and basic entomology, it also has intricate and specialized plays like any other playbook.

This revised *Fly Fisher's Playbook* still supports consistency in planning, rigging, and fundamental skills and techniques that, combined with a systematic approach, will afford you the opportunity to up your angling game. The second edition includes more versatile techniques to assist beginning to advanced fly fishers alike.

My goal when guiding beginners is to help them become self-sufficient fly anglers. When I guide advanced anglers, the emphasis becomes helping to refine their skills and add depth to their arsenal. There are several ways to use a typical or base nymph rig. Over the years I have begun to understand how a simple nymph rig can be used to overcome technical fly fishing. You can make subtle and not so subtle adjustments to the base nymph rig that, quite frankly, most nymph fly fishers don't consider. The playbook will dig deep into those adjustments in an effort to help every nymph fly fisher become more proficient and allow for more hookups on big, selective trout.

The more information you seek, the more you will find. The playbook is ever evolving, as it should be: I learn each and every time out on the water. Since the original book was finished, I have been fortunate enough to hit the river countless times. I still journal, I still learn. This revision of the *Fly Fisher's Playbook* will present the same solid principles associated with nymph fly-fishing techniques and a substantial amount of new information gleaned since the first writing.

As I learn more, I teach more, and as I teach more, I learn more, so I've added a lot to the book. Although it has all of the previous information included in the previous edition, this version of the *Fly Fisher's Playbook* is not the same book, just as the river is not the same river, and I am not the same man. Everything's better.

1

Gear

The gear you choose for nymphing can be a liability or weakness in your playbook. What gear you buy is a personal decision, but selecting the wrong gear can make for long days on the water. Just like you wouldn't use a 6-foot stepladder to replace a lightbulb 10 feet off the ground, you should try to select gear suited for the job. You may be able to change that lightbulb, but not comfortably and certainly not safely.

I always advise people to try everything out before they buy. Fly shops are great about letting you try everything from waders and boots to fly rods. If you don't have a shop near you, try to find people you know who will let you try their gear. Nymphing gear is like anything else you are considering purchasing and using—pick what fits your price and you the best. But remember, you must have the proper tools for the job at hand, so select prudently within the guidelines below.

Which Stick?

Typically, nymphing is easiest to perform with at least a 9-foot fly rod. Anything shorter than that can hamper the cast and drift. A 10-foot fly rod for nymphing can be a great advantage. Too short a fly rod makes it

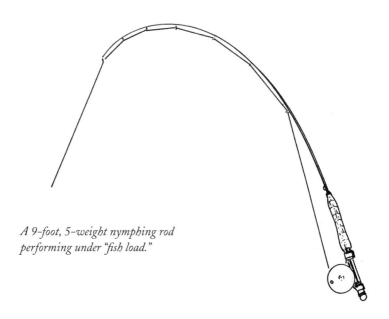

*A 9-foot, 5-weight nymphing rod
performing under "fish load."*

tough to high-stick in many spots and also makes it difficult to perform long-line mending. Advanced anglers can get away with an 8-foot fast-action rod, but most opt for simplicity and use the extra foot. I also recommend a 5-weight rod with medium action. Again, advanced anglers like to fish the faster action rods and lighter weight rods (3-weight or 4-weight), but for nymphing I have found it best to use a 9-foot, 5-weight, medium-action rod. I like the medium- or mid-action rods because they are softer on the set, easy on light tippets, and load perfectly with multiple flies, split shot, and various indicators.

Rods come in a wide range of values and prices. Find a rod in your price range, put some quality floating line on it, and you will be able to be efficient. I prefer a floating line for nymphing with an indicator, because it allows you to form a hinge point below the indicator, thus giving you the ability to dial in your depth, which directly affects your drift efficiency. Anything that comes between you and a good nymph drift hampers your ability to hook fish, which makes you less efficient as a nymph fly fisher. In other words, if you have to overcome a mismatched fly rod to line combo, or fly line that sinks where it's not supposed to, then you're impeding success from the get-go because you have to work harder than you should. In fly fishing, economy of motion, or the ability to fish without wasted motion, is paramount if you want to be on the river all day.

Match your fly line to the weight of your fly rod. On some of the faster action rods, select a line a full weight or half weight above the specs on the fly rod. Remember, in most nymphing situations, you will only be casting 10 to 15 feet of fly line, so some of the fast-action rods need a bit more line weight to load properly. Faster action rods typically have stiffer tips than soft or medium-action rods. Next time you're in a fly shop, try comparing the action of a few different rods and you'll see that some flex closer to the handle than others. Rods with faster action flex farther away from the handle. This leads to a stiffer fly rod that, for shorter casts, could use a bit heavier fly line to help load or bend the rod.

For a 9-foot, 5-weight rod, you can select your line from a bunch of choices. I like a double-taper floating line for most nymphing situations. The biggest reason for a double taper, for me, is that I can flip the line when one end tires out, and bingo, line like new. Again, you're not going to be laying out a bunch of line nymphing, so get something that is versatile and long lasting. For a 5-weight, mid-action rod, I usually select a floating line marked DT5F (double taper, 5-weight, floating). I also like to throw a floating weight-forward line (WF5F or weight forward, 5-weight, floating). This line, because of its forward weight, helps to load faster action fly rods and has a long taper that helps during longline mends. I haven't personally cast lines developed for indicators, but I have had clients fish them. They seem to turn over flies easily because of a thicker head diameter and shorter front taper.

As for fly line color, I think that color choice is for the fisherman and not the fish. Let me explain. If you continually bomb a run with your fly line, sooner or later you're going to put fish down, regardless of color. Some may disagree with me on that theory, but surface disruption of any nature puts down fish. I can think of a couple instances where fly line color may be beneficial to the fly fisher. First is the beginning angler just learning to mend to the drift. In this case, for a brief period of time, it's advantageous for the angler to see the line as he or she mends. Although it's not imperative, the ability to see the line during mending for the beginner flattens out the learning curve because a mended line that is plainly visible reinforces mending techniques. Another instance is for the fly fisher who desires to nymph without an indicator. The ability to see the line, especially the line butt to leader knot, helps when detecting a strike.

This all boils down to using any fly line color you desire, according to your nymphing technique and your skill level. When you learn how to set up properly on a run to minimize spooking fish with your casts, the color of the fly line is not an issue. We will delve into how to approach a run in this manner later.

Reel choice can be just as important as rod and line choice and can easily become a fly-fishing strength. A mismatched reel, line, and rod will reduce economy of motion and become a weakness where it could easily be a strength. The harder you have to work to present your nymph rig, the less efficient you will be and the less fun you will have during outings. Fly fishing can be challenging enough even with well-matched equipment.

Choose something that fits in your price range. A reel is basically nothing more than a line storage device. The first reel my dad gave me when I was 10 years old had no drag system. I was happy with that reel but didn't know how much I didn't know about reels.

Reels come in different finishes, weights, arbor size, and drags, but the three main purposes of a reel remain the same. Reels are designed to store line and backing, provide a smooth drag system, and balance your fly rod.

For nymphing, I like a large arbor reel and a multiplier retrieval system with a disc or conical drag system. The large arbor reel gives me the ability to pick up line fast (spooling), helps smooth out the drag, and reduces tight memory fly line curls. The multiplier retrieval system simply multiplies how much line I gain with each spool revolution, so I can spool line quickly with fewer revolutions or cranks. It's a great physical advantage to be able to collect a lot of line with little effort. The drag system is my personal choice from years of experience.

As for setting your drag, Landon Mayer in a recent article in the *High Country Angler* (winter 2011), outlined how to set your drag so well, that I asked him if I could relay it in this book. He explains that the drag should be set strict enough to be able to lift a fish without the drag releasing, but be set at the proper tension to spool when the fish runs or headshakes. His methods for setting the drag are easy and consistent. He outlined two methods: one that uses a buddy and the other that uses a chair or some other heavy object. Simply apply pressure to the fly line by lifting the fly rod to the maximum flex and set the drag so no line is spooling out. If you have a buddy holding the line, have him or her apply pressure that mimics a fighting fish, and if your drag is set properly, this is the only time line should release from the spool. You can simulate the buddy system by using a chair, and instead of a buddy mimicking a fighting fish, you can simply lift up abruptly on the fly rod while in maximum flex.

There are a lot of reel choices out there, but the characteristics I outlined above give me exactly what I want when I am nymph fishing. Try different reels for your fly rod; you will be amazed at the differences. Lastly, to help prolong the life of your reel disc drag, many reel manufacturers recommend you loosen it when you plan to store your reel for extended periods. This prevents flat spots in any disc drag system and ensures a smooth drag. It's a great habit to develop.

Do These Waders Make My Butt Look Big?

You'll hear a lot of opinions on what gear is best and why, but it comes down to personal choice and functionality. Take waders for example: dozens of different brands, each may suit what you need, but how do you choose? Simply, I look for a wader that is breathable, has a front pocket, comfortable straps, and a built-in wading belt. I have been wearing the same brand for several years, and if I treat them right, I can usually get about 80 trips out of a pair. Pick yourself up a tube of wader repair; I like the stuff that hardens as you expose it to ultraviolet light (like the sun). Try to hang your waders to dry after a day on the water. This will not only discourage mildew but can help discourage the spread of invasive species as well through complete drying.

Boot choice, again, is personal. Get a pair of boots that is a bit oversized if you plan to nymph in winter so you can wear thick socks. Because of invasive species in some waters, you may wish to invest in a pair of rubber Vibram soles because it appeared for a while as if felt soles may get the boot. Recent studies have shown that invasive species like the zebra mussel, quagga mussel, or New Zealand mudsnail can adhere to not only the felt soles on wading boots, but just about anything else with a similar texture. Companies are still producing felt-soled boots, and you should follow a few measures with all gear to aid in preventing the spread of invasive species.

The best ways to help prevent the spread of invasive species through your wading equipment is to either allow a solid five days between trips for equipment to dry completely or dedicate one set of wading equipment per body of water. You can use chemicals like commercial grade 409 on your waders, or deep-freeze them to kill the species, but deep freezing is not an option for me because I need my boots nearly every day. Chemical dips or sprays work fine, but again, the cost and hassle for me to perform this every day would be prohibitive. Heck, most of my wading boots rarely dry out when the season is at full tilt. What I do is buy a different pair of boots and waders for each body of water to ensure I don't spread invasive species. I dedicate a pair of boots and waders to each particular river I guide. For a person who doesn't fly-fish as often, the other methods of control are viable.

I had a conversation with Jeff Spohn, aquatic biologist for Colorado Parks and Wildlife, regarding preventing the spread of invasives. Jeff suggests that anglers thoroughly clean and dry waders and boots, removing all mud or vegetation, and also refrain from moving immediately from one body of water to another. He explained that his usual method of preventing the spread is by freezing his wading equipment overnight. He simply thaws the equipment in the water before putting

Proper waders and boots not only keep you dry, but can also keep you comfortable in winter months.

it on for a day of work. Jeff also liked the idea of a separate set of waders and boots for different bodies of water, but we agree that's not viable for all anglers. Finally, he suggested that each angler chooses his or her own method of proven prevention and sticks with it.

For boot selection, you also have to consider the type of bottom of the river you will be nymphing. Some river bottoms like the South Platte are mostly sand with a few rocks, so you don't need extra traction. Other rivers, like the Blue and Eagle Rivers have a bottom that feels like bowling balls covered with Vaseline. It's super slick and hard to plant your feet. In this case, I'll wear Vibram soles with studs or cleats. I always carry felt-soled boots and studded boots in my truck to accommodate various river bottoms. Just like waders, try several pairs to get the right fit for your buck.

I recently purchased a pair of boots that have sticky rubber soles. This particular pair of boots are stout and lightweight and do in fact have sticky soles. I haven't had to use cleats and still feel comfortable wading. Some commercial cleats work well, and I've known other guides who prefer to use short sheet-metal screws as cleats.

Speaking of wading comfort, more and more of my clients are carrying wading staffs. Most have the compact staff that attaches neatly to a wading belt or wader loop. This way the staff is there when you need it and folds neatly enough that it's not in the way when sheathed. The ability to quickly deploy a third contact point in the river as you wade not only gives peace of mind, but offers more safety. As always, do your homework, and you can find some great products that are perfect for the waters you fish.

As for choosing between a vest or waist pack, most guides I work with use the waist pack. I wore a vest for over 30 years and loved it. About two years ago, the other guides I worked with convinced me to try a waist pack. I purchased a popular brand and immediately began to wear it. I couldn't get used to it. Problem was, I tried to wear it like the young gun guides I hung out with. They could wear theirs without having to use the shoulder strap. Not me: my physique is not what it used to be. Dang thing kept sliding down my hips. I was about ready to can the whole idea and return to my beloved vest when I saw a guide on the river using the shoulder strap. I love my waist pack; it fits me just fine. I will say this: what it feels like in the store is often different from how it feels and performs for you on the river. If you have a buddy who has a particular model, ask to wear it a bit while you fish.

As for tools, I wear a lanyard and I truly recommend a lanyard system; it puts everything right in front of you, while staying out of the way. It simplifies my tool management system. On my lanyard you'll find 3X to 6X tippet, nippers, foam for drying dry flies, floatant, tungsten putty, and an indicator brush. I didn't begin to sport a lanyard until I switched over to a waist pack, and wish I had gone to it sooner. Everything is right in front at your disposal, and I have yet to curse it for being in the way or creating a weakness.

A few other items I don't leave home without are hemostats, split shot (size 6 through BB), thermometer, scissors for trimming yarn

A few favorite and necessary tools.

indicators, and a camera. Some brands of hemostats have scissors built in. I use those exclusively so I don't need to carry scissors for trimming yarn indicators. To help protect my camera from getting dunked, I attach it to a lanyard and hang it around my neck. Although I carry a waterproof camera, I only want it in the water when the time comes. Nothing worse than a water spot on a hero picture. It rides nicely behind the front of my waders and is easy to employ. Choose your items based on personal criteria and what's best for your system.

Two items of utmost importance that I have saved for last are optics and a journal. Your choice of sunglasses is, in my opinion, as important as the fly rod you choose. Maybe more. I like sunglasses that have large side shields to block out the sun and errant flies, with polarized coffee-colored lenses. I feel as if the coffee-colored lenses work in most light conditions. I cannot express enough the importance of good optics. Seeing fish is at least half the battle! I often tell folks that I'm a much better guide and fly fisher when I can spot fish. The ability to see fish before they see you increases the chances for a hookup. The ability to actually watch the fish eat multiplies that tenfold. Good optics will do that for you.

As for a journal, well, it plays an integral role in my fly fishing. I record everything. You can pick up a commercial journal at most fly shops, or you can buy small wire-ring notebooks that fit neatly into a pocket. I record water flows, clarity, weather conditions, flies used, hatches, riseforms, fish caught, barometric pressure, and anything else ordinary and out of the ordinary. My journal has become my playbook.

This journal has evolved over the years. Because I fish one river 90 percent of my guiding days, I have covered not all, but most, of the conditional changes I need to document. Won't say I've seen it all, but I'm fairly sure I've seen most of it on this particular river. What my journal has become is a compilation of one-word descriptors and short accounts of interesting occurrences. The other day, for example, all I wrote was, "Heavy hail, drank a beer under the porch." When I go to a different river to guide, it's back to the old ways, and I diligently record the usual items. It pays dividends.

You want gear that performs correctly; suits your needs, personality, and pocketbook; and is easy to manage. It's the old Ford vs. Chevy argument. Use what suits your nymphing needs best, what matches your strengths best, and what helps you fish with the most confidence. As you evolve as a fly fisher (and believe me, I evolve each time out) your strengths and needs change as your weaknesses diminish. I have tried to give you some basic guidelines for gear and knowledge you can put into play immediately, which can help you manage a simple systematic approach to nymphing. The simpler the system you put into play, the less energy you must focus on distractions, which will in turn, allow you to fish to your strengths, while you work on your weaknesses.

Xs and Os

- Purchase gear for nymphing as outlined above, choosing the types of styles that work best for you.
- The gear you choose can help boost your confidence.
- Keep it simple, and allow your gear to evolve with your expertise.

2

Fish to Your Strengths

My college baseball coach once told me, "Boy, you're small, but you sure are slow." Seems like I had a few shortcomings as a ballplayer, but I kept myself in the lineup by hard practice and a willingness to compete—and I could swing the bat a bit. It's imperative that we work on our weaknesses as we perform to our strengths. In other words, when I played ball, I continued to lift weights and work on foot speed, while swinging the bat and wanting to compete kept me off the bench. I continued to work on fundamentals, which removed distractions by simplifying the game. My goal was to control what I could through learning certain skills and mastering the tools of the trade. The same holds true for fly fishing.

I realized long ago that I am not the best fly fisherman or guide out there. After nearly 47 years toting a fly rod around, I realize there are holes in my game. I also recognize my strengths and continue to chip away at my weaknesses. It's in my playbook—my systematic approach to all facets of fly fishing. I look at one area of weakness at a time and strive to be better today than I was yesterday. It's that systematic approach that has helped me improve over the years. My playbook, or my methods, approach, and strengths and weaknesses, are personal and ever-evolving. We all have our own playbooks, our own methods and strengths and weaknesses. The playbook evolves each time you get out, and I believe if your approach is systematic with an eye toward improving each time out, you will improve quickly.

Scout Yourself

I was a bird dog scout for the Cincinnati Reds for over a decade. I was always looking for that five-tool player to recommend for further scouting and cross-checking. A five-tool player (one who had arm strength, hitting, foot speed, fielding, and baseball acumen) was difficult to find, but finding a three-tool player was a bit easier. I know a bunch of three-tool fly fishers who wish to become five-tool fly fishers. How do you get to that next step?

The first step is realizing that you have holes in your fly fishing. One of the best ways to discern your weaknesses is to scout yourself. The easiest way to do that is to go out with a qualified guide for even half a day. Other ways to get a fix on your weaknesses are to watch fly-fishing shows, go to seminars, pick up a few books or magazines, or fish with someone who's better than you. I always ask clients before the trip what they would like to work on that day. Most folks have a pretty good idea of areas they wish to work on or areas in their game that need work; some aren't completely sure and say they want to catch more fish on a regular basis.

I'm fine with whatever folks say, but on average, the clients who have an area they want to work on, or who have scouted themselves, are typically further along in the process. With clients who fall in the second category, we will fish a bit, and then I'll tell them what we will really work on that day. I'll put a name to it and refer to it throughout our time on the water. Once you name a weakness, you can begin to correct it and turn it into strength. Be honest with yourself.

Weaknesses

Let's break down several weaknesses I see on a frequent basis. Some of these I will discuss in depth in coming chapters; some I'll take a poke

By honestly evaluating the holes in your game, you can improve quickly.

at right now. These are weaknesses that are easy to work on. Learning the fixes will add versatility to your playbook and eventually make fly fishing much more enjoyable. My goal is to help you turn what seems like a weakness into a strength and to give you not only the skills to increase your daily hookups, but also the ability to progress through options as you nymph-fish.

Knots

If you fish frequently, I am sure you have walked past that poor soul who has his or her nose stuck into a terrible bird's nest of flies, leader, and tippet. I learned long ago that when the tangle becomes that snarled, the best thing to do is snip off your bugs, salvage what you can, and retie. A lot of folks don't want to do that because they aren't profi-cient at tying knots. How about fishing all day, finally setting the hook on a nice fish only to have a knot fail? Knots are simple, they are something you can improve quickly, and they shouldn't be a weakness.

You'll find a ton of knot-tying information online or through other resources. It's relatively simple to practice knot tying. When I teach fly-fishing classes we use $1/8$-inch nylon cord and large eyebolts to learn and practice knots. This practice transfers neatly to leaders and tippets with a little work.

The main knots you need for nymphing are the clinch knot (fly to leader or tippet), the surgeon's knot (leader to tippet), the blood knot (leader to tippet), and the perfection loop (leader to fly line). Don't limit yourself there, but continue to add other knots to your playbook arsenal, such as the nail knot, the knots used to attach fly line to your backing (Albright knot), and backing to your fly reel (arbor knot). Remember to lubricate your knots with spit before tightening them. If a knot squeaks as you tighten it, redo it. Just that little bit of friction can weaken the knot to the point it will fail. The more you can add to your playbook, the more efficient and proficient you become.

The Importance of Nymphing

Some folks are great streamer fly fishers; others are great at dry-fly fishing. I think you'll pick up more fish on a regular basis by nymphing. I've heard estimates that a fish eats 90 percent of its diet subsurface. I like ripping fish on dries and dry-dropper rigs, and using streamers to locate fish or to prefish new areas before guiding, but my bread is buttered by subsurface nymphing. I always encourage folks to work on their nymphing skills to increase their enjoyment of the sport. I think all types of fly fishing are fine, and they complement one another. If nymphing is a weakness, I certainly encourage you to become proficient.

"I've always done it this way." I hear that a bunch. I wouldn't dare change the throwing motion of a great pro quarterback, but if he is less than stellar, I wouldn't hesitate to offer suggestions. Be open to suggestions and constructive criticism.

When my dad first put a fly rod in my hand, he taught me to watch the nail knot to detect strikes. I danced around not using indicators for twenty years but finally used one on a guide trip down the North Platte many years ago. Wow, I was missing a lot of fish.

Engage and Experiment

Learn to take chances and experiment a bit. A couple of winters ago, I started fiddling around with dead drifting squirrel tail leech patterns below an indicator. It opened up a whole new world for me. So, try adding experimentation to your playbook.

I find it intriguing to watch the posture of those I'm guiding throughout the day. If we go through a lull in the action, folks naturally change their posture. They, in essence, become spectators instead of players. Then, after we hook up, their posture changes, they lean into the drift, and they begin to set on every little bump, twitch, and pause. Stay focused even when the action is sparse. Fish like a ninja. A good friend and fellow guide, Jesse Bertsch, is a fly-fishing ninja. He always leans in to his indicator, he moves a bit after every few casts or so, and he is absolutely a fish-bomber. He guides the same way. You look at Jesse and his clients as they fish, and everyone is leaning in, anticipating a strike, and attentive. Posture is something you can improve the next time out.

See 'Em and Cast to 'Em

Half the battle for becoming a better fly fisher is the ability to spot fish. I am amazed at some of the guides I work with. They spot fish like an osprey. Good sunglasses are important, no doubt, but so is the ability to read the water and knowing the areas fish like to hold. Once you begin to sight-fish regularly, you learn how to sight-nymph, how to position yourself for casting, and how to control your profile. We will discuss this in depth in the chapter dealing with strategies, but if this is a weakness for you, it needs to be addressed quickly.

Some claim that there is a difference between being able to cast and being able to fish. Although I agree, I have found over the years that most folks who cast well, fish well. You don't have to be a certified caster to nymph proficiently, but the ability to roll cast, full cast, and add a reach mend certainly comes in handy when you are nymphing. Being able to put your indicator and flies relatively close to your target and do it without creating a huge tangle is imperative to nymphing. I'll discuss this more later, but suffice it to say, if you can hit your target, and nymph-fish tangle-free, you are way ahead of the game.

Learn Your Bugs

One of the most common weaknesses I see in anglers is that they have difficulty identifying and matching aquatic insects. Yes, I'm referring to the *e* word, *entomology*. When I teach my classes I watch for students' eyes to begin to glaze over. Not because the information is boring, but it can become tedious. There is a lot to learn about bugs. Approach this as you would any weakness in your game. Work to learn as much as possible, and then marry this information to reading the water, fish behavior, how to tie your nymph rig, and the drift. We will dig into this more later. It's really not that cumbersome; you'll see.

Take a Breather

One of the biggest weaknesses I see when working with clients, or when fishing around other folks, is that they don't seem to be enjoying themselves. I have never caught a trout in an ugly place. My friend Chris Harrison once told me of a time he was fishing with his dad. After some time in the water, Chris said to his dad something along the lines of, "Gee, I ought to stop fishing so hard, and take a look around." To which his dad replied, "I ought to stop looking around and get to fishing!" A while back, I was lucky enough to guide an eight-year-old boy and his dad. We'd been fishing a while and enjoying success when out of the blue the boy asked me if I could see the ape on the mountain. I was totally engrossed in following his indicator, and this snapped my head up. "What ape, where?" "The ape just below the iguana," he says nodding toward Long Scraggy View Mountain. I look

Soak it all in. Can you see the ape and the iguana?

at that nearly every day as a reminder to look around more and soak it all in. Sometimes I get so engrossed in just catching fish that I miss the best part of the activity. Sure, I want to catch fish as much or more than the next guy, but I have learned balance. It's about the entire outdoor experience. Enjoy it—it beats work every time.

Three or so years ago, my good friend and fellow guide Jack Moreno and I were doing some research and development on the South Platte. Let's face it—we were fishing. I was fishing ahead of Jack, and we were throwing similar rigs. I stopped at a run that had a little riffle, which filtered into a decent plunge pool in front of a huge rock.

Jack was having a good day, cleaning up fish behind me at about a three-to-one ratio. I was feeling anxious because he was schooling me even though I was getting first crack at the runs. I began to fish too quickly, shortening my drifts, casting too far, and always looking upstream to find a spot where the fishing would be better. I placed two or three less-than-perfect drifts through that plunge pool and moved to the riffle above because it looked better. I was on a mission. Jack proceeded to step into that hole and catch 13 fish on 13 consecutive casts. I was hot but realized a valuable lesson. I shouldn't have been competing with Jack, when in essence I am competing with the fish.

I am all for healthy competition, but when clients or buddies begin competing, the quality of the entire experience is lost. When players don't perform well in pressure situations it's often referred to as choking—and it's hard to fly-fish with both hands on your own throat. Call a time-out. Relax. Now when I guide through that run that we affectionately named "Butt Kickin' Rock," I remember the lesson I learned about how competition can cloud the way I, and other folks, approach the river. By the way, I returned the favor to Jack last year on Spinney Mountain Ranch. Who, me, competitive? Yup, but I truly strive to minimize the effects of this weakness.

Up Your Game Quickly

Clients ask me all the time about how they can become better quicker. After I state the obvious answer about research, classes, watching videos, and such, I always explain to them to try to learn one section of a river. Find one section of home water, and fish it through four seasons, especially winter. With familiarity and confidence comes success, and confidence will transfer to other rivers.

I think that not fishing through the winter months is a weakness. With lower flows, clear water, smaller bugs, and spooky fish, you can accelerate your learning curve markedly. Hire a guide if you need to, but get out there and learn how to fish tricky conditions. Plus, with skinny water conditions, you will be able to find every rock, log, shelf, and bar in a section. Once you master that section, you can begin to expand your section boundaries, and even begin to apply your learning to other rivers. Layer up, find a tailwater, and fish through a season, especially winter.

To take this one step further, let's assume you can handle the fly rod well, drift efficiently, and read the water. You're fishing a run with a buddy who consistently catches more fish than you do. He consistently picks up three fish to every one of yours even though you are rigged similarly and are throwing the same bug patterns. What gives? More than likely, your depth or speed is off. Or maybe he is fishing the water more efficiently, picking it apart piece by piece. Stop, observe, swallow your pride, and ask questions. Why not?

In the above example, the strengths are obvious; it's the weaknesses that need addressing. As you continue to improve, you will begin to fish to your strengths while minimizing your weaknesses. You will begin to overcome holes in your game quickly, which in turn puts more fish in the net. Seriously scout yourself. Set short-term and long-term goals. Try to pick one weakness to work on each time out, and pick a long-term goal you'd like to achieve over a season. Fish to your strengths as you overcome weaknesses, and things will begin to fall into place. That's what it's all about.

Xs and Os

- Scout yourself to find holes in your game.
- Learn and master basic nymph-rig knots.
- Keep an open mind.
- Learn to fish ninja-style.
- Develop the ability to spot fish.
- Develop solid casting skills.
- Manage competitive weaknesses.
- Fish a river section through four seasons.
- Have fun!

3

The Basic Nymph Rig

In football, in order for a team to be competitive, it has to have a good offensive line. These big guys have to be able to meet the defense head on, while opening holes and defending the quarterback. They are the foundation of the team. Without a good foundation, you can have all the skilled players in the world and still struggle to be successful. So it goes for the basic nymph rig. You can be skilled in other areas of your fly fishing, but if you don't have a strong base for your offense, you will struggle at nymphing techniques.

Why give the trout any more advantage than they already have? Setting up properly before you hit the water lets you adjust quickly and efficiently. If I set up correctly to begin with, adjustments I have to make on the water are typically minute. I may only have to tweak weight and depth the rest of the day.

I strongly encourage you to try my setup method for nymphing; however, I understand there are other ways to set up a nymph rig. Whichever way you choose to set up, stick with it for a while. Consistency is important to your nymphing success, and if you continually change methods, you will never realize the advantages and disadvantages of each method. Try my method for a year, and you'll get to know it so well that the adjustments will become second nature.

I have found over the years that my rig is one of the most versatile nymph rigs going. The rig gives you the option to work any and all water columns and the surface film, and you can sight-nymph anything from riffles and pockets to pools. Once you become comfortable with the rig and can quickly and confidently work a stream, you will realize how simple and effective it is.

Rigging the Rig

Take a decent 9-foot, 5-weight fly rod, equipped with floating line that you can effectively roll cast. Next, affix a $7^1/2$-foot, 5X monofilament or fluorocarbon leader to the fly line. I like to use a nail knot for this junction, but other knots work well too. In most places where I guide and fish, a $7^1/2$-foot leader is more than enough to get my rig to the depths required. Sometimes, however, a 9-foot leader is called for. Remember, the longer the leader, the longer the distance between the weight and the indicator, which can make it difficult to quickly set on a fish eating. You need fast reflexes, but you also need to make a long, sweeping motion to take up all the line in order to set the hook. I haven't run into too many situations where I have had to use a 9-footer because I add up to 18 inches of tippet to the end of the $7^1/2$-foot leader. After adding the lengths of tippet between each fly, you get a total depth of nearly 11 feet. That's suitable for most nymphing out West.

Here's a quick tip: so that I can make quick leader replacements or changes when a leader is worn out, instead of retying a nail knot, I sometimes leave the nail knot attached to the fly line, cut and leave about 10 inches of leader butt section, and tie a perfection loop at the end of it. With the perfection loop in place, I can quickly attach another leader with a loop-to-loop connection while on guided trips. Make sure you pull the loop-to-loop connection tight in order to flatten the profile of the knots to keep them out of the way. As with all knots, make sure they don't have a large-profile knot or any long tag ends that will reach out and tangle everything.

To the end of your leader you need to tie on monofilament (mono) or fluorocarbon (fluoro) 5X tippet. If you are using a 4X leader, you can attach 4X tippet or step down to 5X if conditions dictate. Consider water flow and clarity, the size flies you are using, the substrate you are fishing, and the size of fish you are targeting when choosing your tippet size. Typically, the rougher and rockier the substrate, the bigger and nastier the water, and the bigger fish get the heavier tippets. If I'm not using heavier tippets, then I rig 5X fluoro for pretty much every situation. Use a double surgeon's knot or a blood knot and tie on about 16 to 18 inches of tippet. I tie on a minimum of 16 inches of tippet when I begin the day knowing that I will eat some of that length up as the day goes on just switching out or retying flies. The best length of tippet is usually about 14 to 16 inches, and I replace the entire tippet once it gets down to about a foot. You can tie on a monofilament leader and attach fluorocarbon tippet. In this case it's best to use a triple surgeon's knot. Because of their different characteristics, sometimes fluoro and mono don't play well together. Fluorocarbon has a tendency to want to cut through monofilament. The third loop on the triple surgeon's knot helps absorb some of the abrasive qualities of fluorocarbon line. Lubricate all knots well before you tighten them.

Next, tie on your first fly, or your dropper, to the end of the tippet with a clinch knot or improved clinch knot. I typically tie the simple clinch knot here; it works fine if you tie it properly. We'll discuss fly choice at length later. I recommend using at least a two-fly rig, so at this point you'll tie more tippet to either the eye or the hook bend of the dropper. I use a simple rule to determine if I want to tie to the eye or bend of the dropper. If I tie the next section of tippet to the eye, I tend to get a bug that's cruising in a flat profile through the water. Conversely, if I tie to the bend of the hook, my fly will have a tendency to tumble through the water.

I ask myself, does the bug I'm trying to match swim well? For example, a big Golden Stonefly nymph can't swim worth a darn, and I have never seen one floating headfirst down the river. I will tie it eye to bend to assist in getting the proper drift profile. On the other hand, if I am fishing, say, a nymph or emerger that can swim, like a BWO nymph, I'll tie it eye to eye to flatten out the profile.

Now you have tied the leader to the tippet, and the tippet to the dropper fly. It's time to tie on our last fly, or the point fly. This is a fly you tie to the eye of the hook only using a clinch knot. In a two-fly nymph rig, I use 12 to 14 inches of tippet between my dropper and point flies. If I decide to throw a three-fly rig, I reduce the distance between bugs to 8 to 10 inches. I do this because I want to be able to effectively manage a three-bug rig, and reducing the distance between them not only reduces the amount of line I have to cast, mend, and set, but it reduces the distance a trout has to move from side to side to eat my offering. Sounds nitpicky, but we want to take any advantage away from the fish.

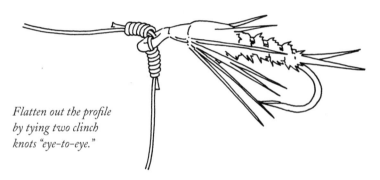

Flatten out the profile by tying two clinch knots "eye-to-eye."

Cadence

Most of my clients raise an eyebrow when I finish tying their three-bug nymph rig. They often will ask if they will be able to effectively fish it. My motto is, "If you can say three-bug rig, you can certainly fish it." It simply comes down to slowing down your tempo or nymphing cadence. I've started to notice that when my clients are fishing well and picking up fish they get into a rhythm. The drift is solid, and the position set employed at the end of each drift (see page 72) becomes the beginning of the next drift. It's like a mathematical equation—each

Matching the rhythm and river cadence can lead to catching fine fish

part is important and builds a base for the next step. You become part of the water, get in tune with the rhythm, and make subtle changes in the drift mechanics and angles that make the flies come alive.

The cadence doesn't only benefit the drift; it allows you to manage five hinge points, weight, and an indicator when casting. Whether you are using a full cast or a simple roll cast, the ability to slow down is important. When I am struggling with cadence, I simply remind myself to make each cast—and each drift—count. One at a time, stack good casts and drifts like cordwood, and your playbook will become much more versatile.

Profiles

Let's back up a bit before we finish setting up our rig. Some fly fishers tie all of their droppers eye to eye because they feel it lessens the chance for the fish to feel the tippet as they eat. I am not in that camp. If fish eat your nymph as it comes downstream to them, they will feel the line regardless of where it's tied to the hook. Even if a fish swings on the fly as it drifts by, and eats it going away, it will most likely feel the line. My point of view is that even if an eye-to-eye connection does what some say, I would rather match the profile of a drifting bug and increase the chance that it will spur a fish into eating. Fish eat and spit so quickly that I cannot be sure the fish spit the bug because it felt the tippet; therefore, I'll take my chances and try to get the profile I want.

More Rigging and Reality

Remember the leader-to-tippet connection we made? Now it's time to place a split shot above it. That knot will also serve to keep your weight from sliding down the tippet toward your dropper. The size of split shot is determined by factors like water depth, speed, and so on, and we will get into that formula later.

After you place the weight, you can affix an indicator to the leader. The rule of thumb for the indicator is to place it $1^1/2$ times the depth of the water you are fishing. So in 3 feet of water, set the indicator 5 feet from your weight. I go a step further and call it the reality rule. Is the weight really on the bottom? Because of water speeds and other sub-surface factors, most of the time the $1^1/2$ rule does not get the job done. Recognizing this is what separates the advanced nymph fly fishers from everyone else. There's no excuse for not setting the depth correctly because you can see the weight ticking on the bottom. You can observe the weight bouncing on the bottom transferred up to the indicator.

When working with clients, I often suggest that after working a run, we step in to see just how deep it is and compare the depth and

*A fishing-ready, trimmed, and
floatant-dressed yarn indicator.*

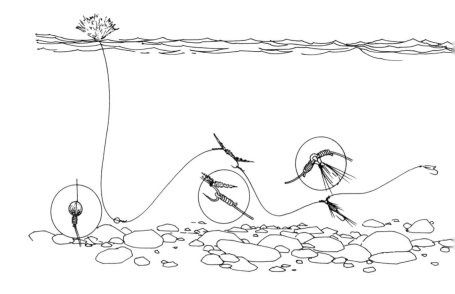

A typical rig set-up like the one you see here is quick, versatile, and effective.

water speeds with the distance we set the indicator from the weight. Often, they are amazed at how much more distance we have than the $1^{1}/_{2}$ rule. It's all about hydraulics, water speeds, and casting angles. When you have the right depth, you'll know it. Everything slows down, and intuitively you know you're in the zone.

You have to adjust the indicator depth throughout the day, so pick an indicator you can see, one that holds your rig up, *and* one that's easy to move quickly. I am a big fan of a yarn indicator attached to the leader with a small rubber band. It's quick and easy to move, it floats all day when dressed properly, and you can trim the profile as needed. This indicator type is also sensitive to any take.

Other types of indicators work just as well, but I like that I can trim the yarn to a profile that I like. I have recently begun to incorporate two different colors into one indicator. I think the contrasting colors make it easier to recognize subtle takes. Experiment with all the types of indicators, and choose the one you like best.

That's it. If you have followed the guidelines above, you have created a simple nymph rig that is easy to manage, versatile, and quick to adjust. Make an effort to use this nymph rig over time. The more you use it, the more you will be able to estimate where the flies are in relation to the indicator. You'll be able to accurately judge where your flies are in each portion of the nymph drift. That's huge. If you know where and how fish are feeding and where your bugs are, you are certainly going the right direction. You'll see in the coming chapters why I set my rigs this way. It's the basis for my approach to nymphing—my big ole offensive line.

Xs and Os

- The basic nymphing rig needs to be simple and easy to adjust.
- Correctly setting up the rig is critical to your success.
- Consider the bugs' profile in the river when choosing the knots you tie to droppers.
- The basic nymph rig is the basis for your playbook.
- Develop a nymphing cadence.

4

Survey the Defense

I was recently guiding on the South Platte when I spotted a nice fish in a far seam tucked between two trees, neatly situated beside a boulder—a pretty nifty prime lie for a dominant rainbow. This particular fish was in the middle column actively feeding on *Baetis* emergers. My client and I eased our way out of the river to the bank to set up for this fish.

Since we were running a nymph rig under a yarn indicator, we had some adjustments to make. I quickly removed the Pheasant Tail Nymph, tied on a Barr Emerger to simulate the size and stage of the bug the fish was munching, adjusted for less depth, and removed some weight. We snuck in from a downstream angle, laid out the correct amount of line downstream, and my client placed a short, leader-first upstream cast about three feet above the fish. As if it read the script, the rainbow ate that bug on the first drift.

That is just one example of surveying or reading the defense and making adjustments to collect a fish. When I am on the water, I am constantly surveying the defense. It's not unusual for me to stand at the river's edge looking things over before I even put my first rig on for the day. What am I looking for? I always look at river flows (cubic feet per second or cfs), water clarity and temperature, and weather forecasts

Alan Peak surveying the defense before attacking the river.

(temperature, wind, fronts). I then marry that information to seasonal bug hatches, flows and temperatures (air and water), angling pressure, trout feeding patterns and locations, and any other factors that can contribute to trout defense.

A trout's defense is anything that gives the fish a distinct advantage or factors that impede its interest in eating your offering. Just yesterday a client and I were sneaking up on a feeding rainbow that was situated on a sand flat: a perfect setup for us to get a crack at this bruiser. Just before we began to sneak back out of the willows to begin our pursuit, I noticed an eagle flying toward us down the river. We froze as the eagle flew directly over us. I paid close attention to the fish and thought all was well as the eagle had passed well beyond us. Just then, because of the angle of the sun, I noticed the eagle's shadow pass directly over the fish. I thought that fish was going to turn inside out as it scrambled to get out of there! Yup, even an eagle can serve as a defense for a fish.

Water Temperature

I am concerned with water temperatures. If you look at my fly-fishing journals from over the years, you will notice I record detailed temperature data. The rule of thumb is that hot water equals less oxygen for trout and that cold water equals more oxygen for trout. Remember this, and remember what water temperatures provide the best feeding windows for the trout species you're targeting. Let's dig into temperatures for a bit.

Rainbow trout prefer cold, clear water with a temperature range of 55 to 60 degrees. When spawning, the optimum temperatures are between 44 and 50 degrees. From 32 to 44 degrees, fish metabolism slows and they don't require much food. Tailwaters can be the exception here as they typically flow colder. From 50 to 55 degrees, you can expect good feeding activity over longer durations, including tailwaters, with 55 to 65 degrees being the optimum on freestones. In skinny or shallow waters and some smaller tailwaters, the 55- to 65-degree range can begin to turn off the feeding activity. Here's the kicker (and there's always a kicker): I've caught river rainbows from the low 30-degree range to the high 60-degree range. What temperature ranges that are best for the rivers you fish may be different because of seasonal and river variables.

On tailwaters (rivers that originate from a dam or tail from a dam), there are other factors to consider. Typically, these waters are colder simply because they originate from a reservoir. However, how deep the reservoir is, and where water displacement occurs from the dam, plays an important role in the temperature downstream. Some dams spill water through tubes or gates at the base of the dam, allowing the cold water from the lowest level of the reservoir to create the flow. Some dams spill from the middle of the dam, sending the midlevel temperatures of the reservoir to create the flow. And some dams truly spill water over the top of the dam, allowing the reservoir's warmest water to create the flow.

Seasonally, some dams spill over the top *and* from the bottom tubes, thus mixing the water and giving a modified temperature flow.

This usually occurs during runoff when there's too much water behind the dam and substantial amounts of water need to be released. Makes it easy to recognize the variables here, doesn't it? The key is to be able to take and keep accurate temperatures and adjust your fly fishing to the various temperatures of a tailwater.

Because I do most of my fishing on tailwaters, you can see why I keep accurate temperature data. It's important to take this data for all four seasons you fish a particular tailwater or freestone. I know that in the winter months guiding on the South Platte, the water temperatures have to hit the magic 38.5 degrees before the fish will begin to eat in earnest. Danny Brennan of Flies and Lies in Deckers, Colorado, used to always tell me to be patient and fish until the river hit that magic number. Gotta tell you, he is right. Freestones have a tendency to freeze more readily in the winter and usually have a tougher go of it during runoff, but the temperature range models still hold true.

As for the upper end of the temperature spectrum, I always become concerned, whether on a tailwater or freestone river, when the temperatures start pushing 66 degrees. The trout will still eat, but I am leery of hooking, fighting, landing, taking a picture, and releasing a fish at temperatures on the upper scale. That's why, in the hot summer months, I like to begin trips early and get off of the water before temperatures become dangerous to fish. Remember, high temperatures equal less oxygen, so if you do hook and land a fish, take your time reviving it. Make sure it swims away on its own power, and keep an eye on it if you can. Better yet, when it gets dangerously hot for the fish (upper 60s), go skinny-dipping!

I don't have any data to support my next idea other than my notes, which over the years show that trout have feeding spurts *as* the water moves toward the optimum temperatures. Let's say you get on the river early in the morning and the temperature is 48 degrees. You are picking up fish sporadically but still rolling a few. The sun begins to hit your stretch and begins to push the temperature up a few degrees in a relatively short period of time. As the water nears and hits the magic number, let's say 50 degrees, you notice the feeding activity accelerates.

The same, I believe, is true for late afternoon fishing. You've been picking up an odd fish here or there in the 55-degree range, and as the sun begins to set, the water begins to cool fairly fast, and bingo, fishing picks up again. I've witnessed it countless times. I also think that's why fishing can improve during a brief rain shower; again, as the water cools, the fishing picks up. So in short, stay on that stretch you've been fishing, continue to monitor temperatures, and allow the temperature fluctuations to come into play.

If you don't already have one, a quality thermometer will pay for itself quickly. I use a little infrared gadget a client gave me that takes water temperature simply by pointing it at the water and pushing a button. It's about the size of a ChapStick tube and works great. I can take readings quickly, and after cross-checking my readings with a plunge thermometer, I can verify its accuracy. I use a plunge thermometer below the surface in conjunction with the point-and-shoot thermometer to ensure I'm getting accurate subsurface readings. I have found over the years that the infrared thermometer is quickly getting surface temps that are usually only two or three degrees above the water temps I get about a foot below the surface. After using this method of measurement for years, I no longer cross-check temperatures because I am able to accurately estimate the temperatures underwater. Purchase a small booklet or a commercial fishing journal that can fit into your vest or waist pack, and you're on your way to tracking temperatures.

Water Clarity

Water clarity is easy to ascertain quickly, and it makes a huge difference in fly selection and size, along with leader and tippet selection. During high runoff, which will influence clarity directly, the fish tend to get pushed to the edges of the river. Concentrate on depth and weight as you nymph the edges. Generally, it takes much more weight than in normal water conditions to get to the fish, so don't be afraid to load up. The extra weight will slow that indicator down so you can dredge the bottom. I always imagine the fish wearing goggles and a respirator during these conditions because of the silt, sand, and debris they must endure. Remember, they are still eating, so run big bugs with contrasting colors slowly, and you can pick up fish. Match the bigger flies with heavier leader (7½ foot 3X) and tippet (3X) and increase the size of your indicator to hold all of that up. Monofilament leaders and tippet are fine for these conditions.

On the other side of the spectrum is low, clear water, water that you typically find during late fall, winter, and early spring before runoff. In low, clear conditions, you have to be stealthier. A lot of folks recommend longer leaders during low and clear water conditions. I'm not one of them. If you learn to properly set up on a fish in these conditions and to properly present your flies, there is no need to use a leader longer than 7½ feet. When you add 18 inches of tippet material to the end of your leader, you still are throwing 9 feet of clear line at the fish. I do, however, think you need to reduce the leader and tippet size. In low, clear conditions, I like to rig up with a 7½-foot, 5X or 6X leader with either 5X or 6X tippet. I don't generally use 7X tippet because I feel as if I can use a 5X fluorocarbon and get the same advantage.

This is a good time to talk about monofilament vs. fluorocarbon. Now I'm not super intelligent; as a matter of fact, my claim to educational fame is that I was the tallest kid in third grade for three years running. I tie my rigs with monofilament leaders and tippets 90 percent of the time. The only times I use fluorocarbon leaders and tippet is when I am fishing highly pressured fish or very clear, low water or when I am having difficulty loading enough weight on my rig to get my bugs down quickly. Fluorocarbon or fluoro reflects less light than monofilament line and is effective in very clear water.

Monofilament or nylon leaders have a specific gravity of roughly 1.1, while fluorocarbon has a specific gravity of about 1.75. Since water has a specific gravity of 1.0, you can see that fluorocarbon sinks at a faster rate. That's why I use fluorocarbon when I need to get the flies down quickly, such as fishing a deep shelf just below a fast riffle. Like I mentioned earlier, because it reflects less light, I will use it on heavily pressured fish as well. Because it is more abrasion-resistant than monofilament, I also use it on certain waters where all the rocks seem to have razor edges.

I believe that monofilament tapered leaders, if chosen properly, can do everything I need them to do in presenting a nymph, such as absorb the energy of the fly line and turn over and present the fly naturally. How do you choose the leader? You've got to factor in your fly rod, whether it's fast, medium, or slow action; your casting prowess or style; how far you have to cast; and the defense (weather, clarity, targeted fish, and so on). I always use monofilament leaders for the qualities listed above and for their versatility. If I need to quickly switch out to other modes of rigging, mono suits me well. If I need a bit more invisibility, I'll still throw mono, but I'll use fluoro tippets.

Clients ask me frequently, "How far can you cast?" I always mumble something along the lines that I won't win any casting competitions, but I'm pretty good at a 15-foot roll cast for nymphing. A good monofilament leader works great for most nymphing situations. Essentially, the leader and tippet size is directly proportional to the water conditions, casting needs, and fish targeted (big fish require heavier leader and tippet) in nymphing situations.

That's enough about mono and fluoro leaders for now. Other factors contribute to poor water clarity like a rainstorm, snowmelt from a nearby road or field, and when the lake above the dam turns over. Lakes usually turn over twice a year and can cause the water clarity to become cloudy and cause the water to go "off." Whatever the reason for it, water clarity is an important part of trout defense, and you should be able to switch tactics to overcome it.

River Flows

River flows can be an absolute pain in the neck for those who guide or fish tailwaters regularly. But they do force me to stay sharp. Flows can also pose problems for freestone rivers as well, but they seem to be more seasonal and not a function of a call for water downstream. Most tailwaters are actually glorified irrigation ditches that we just happen to be able to fish. For that I am thankful. When the flows continually move up and down, it's difficult to stay dialed in on the trout holds and feeding patterns.

Tailwaters rise or drop as demand for water increases or decreases for irrigation (industry) or public use. In Western states water is such a valuable resource the old saying "Whiskey's for drinkin' and water's for fightin'" was born. Consumption needs make the flow variable. As the river rises or drops, water temperatures, flows, clarity, and river characteristics fluctuate, and fish move to more advantageous hold areas. They have to keep aligning themselves with food conveyor belts, best oxygenated waters, and adequate shelter.

A few years back I guided on the South Platte as it flowed around 220 cfs. The next morning before I left for my trip to the same water, I called in only to find the river had been bumped to over 600 cfs! Now the fish are still in the river, but not only do you have to adjust your rig and flies, you have to locate the fish. You have to be able to reread the water (see page 42) in a run you just recently fished.

As flows are bumped or dropped by less than 50 cfs, you typically won't have many issues with clarity. On the bigger bumps, it's not uncommon for the river to lose clarity and bring debris downstream. It's not a bad idea to get into the habit of calling in or viewing river flows online before you head out, or stop in to the nearest fly shop and ask. If you're in an area like Cheesman Canyon, where you would have to walk a long way if you get stuck on the other side of the river during a bump, it's a good idea to find a water reference mark as you begin your day. Keep an eye on that reference, especially during seasons of heavy water usage downstream. River flow bumps and drops can add to trout defense, so again, knowing how to react to different flows is critical for success.

I like to nymph in water that is off-color and running higher than normal. If I had my druthers, I'd fly-fish in higher, slightly off-color water every day. It's great for nymphing because fish have less time to inspect your flies, forcing them to make a split decision whether to eat or not. I have found that not only does higher water force fish to the edges, but it will spread them out more evenly over a run as they move to alternate holding spots. Bigger fish will often move into what I call night holds. These are holds that fish move into under the cover of darkness because of feelings of security. Off-color water gives them the same sense of security, so make sure you fish your way into every run when these conditions are present. I'm talking about fishable off-color higher flows, not blowout water conditions. Since tailwaters don't blow out often, one rarely has a day he can't fly fish below a dam.

Weather

I have to be honest with you—although I've done research on weather patterns and the effects on game and fish, I don't have many facts to back up my theories beyond my own observations as a guide. However, I believe that barometric pressure has an effect on fish activity. The anatomy of a fish leads me to believe rising and falling barometer pressures must have an effect on them. Fish have a swim bladder that controls buoyancy. The swim bladder expands and contracts the gas within when a fish moves up or down in the water. I think that barometric pressure may affect feeding activity because of the expanding and contracting of the swim bladder as the pressure goes up or down.

During my research, I discovered that many scientists don't put much stock in the effects of barometer pressures and fish feeding activities. I guide with some of the best guides around, in my estimation, and talk of weather fronts and barometric pressures always comes back to how feeding activity picks up as the barometer is falling as a storm front nears. My own journal reflects this as well. As to the degree that it affects fishing, I can't begin to quantify. Furthermore, my journal reflects that my fishing is fairly stable during a stable or slightly fluctuating barometer and is slightly off after a front as the barometer is rising when it may take a few days to return to normal.

Whatever you believe, understand that this trout defense may affect your fly-fishing success, and put it in your playbook. For me, I have to guide in all conditions anyway, so it doesn't necessarily change the way I approach the defense. I certainly don't tell my clients, "Well, the barometer is rising today, so I don't think we should even get out of the truck." I don't think that would go over too well.

Other weather factors become part of the trout's defense, such as air temperatures, sky conditions, precipitation, and that dirty four-letter word, wind. As for air temperature, on the rivers I fish, water temperature affects the fishing, air temperature affects the fisherman. I know a ton of folks who fly-fish during winter months because it can be stellar and crowds are few. Fishing the tailwaters is popular because the air temperature may be 20 degrees and the water temperature 39 degrees. If you can keep ice out of the fly rod guides, and are dressed properly, it makes for a fine day.

Last winter I spent many days on the river filming an instructional DVD on nymphing. In several of the shots, we had a light snow falling. We have several nice fish on film. Just like a light snowfall, a light rain is easy to fish through, too, provided you are dressed properly. The small amount of precipitation typically doesn't negatively affect the fly fishing. In fact, as I alluded to earlier, a light rain can spur feeding because of the water temperature change. Downpours are another story.

In some cases a downpour can spell the end of the day if small creeks, roads, and hillsides begin to flood. Be careful in those situations, as they can be life threatening. Watch out for lightning too. If the downpour is brief, larger bugs that don't swim well (stonefly nymphs, crane-fly nymphs) or worm patterns work well, because the eroding river edges and increase in water flow may dislodge those bugs from their usual holds.

I have found the old adage that overcast skies can spur bug hatches and fish feeding to be true. But that's not the only advantage of fly fishing under cloudy skies. The fish tend to move into shallower feeding lanes and stay there longer because of the added security of a cloudy sky and the fact that the water may hold cooler temperatures for longer durations than if the sun is high and hot. Also, you can be a lot stealthier without throwing shadows over the water and the bright reflections off your fly rod as you cast. If you are on the water when the sun is high and hot, look for fish in deeper oxygenated water, around or near underwater obstructions and weed beds, or under the shade of streamside vegetation.

And then there's wind. Danny Brennan explains that fishing during heavy wind you need to "mend three times: once for the water, twice for the wind." Wind can certainly put a damper on your day as a fly fisherman. Not too long ago, I had a client plant a size 16 Buckskin firmly in my cheek because a gust of wind hit just as he began to roll-cast. Nice ornament, but it's hard to hook fish when your fly is in somebody's face. Wind serves as a great defense for fish. It's hard to place casts with accuracy, wind knots are prevalent, and it's just plain uncomfortable to fish in. On the positive side (and there's not much positive), a wind can provide a bit of chop on the river that can impede a fish's ability to see you as well as in more placid conditions. Wind may also stir water up on the edges on bigger rivers and provide more food like worms for fish, but I'd still rather fish without wind.

It's fairly easy to see how a fish's defense can be bolstered by a lot of variables that we have no control over. Instead of throwing my hands up in disgust and looking for excuses, I try to circumvent the defense and use options that I've developed over the years to combat the advantages of those variables. As you fish through the four seasons, you can begin to develop your own playbook, with options—not guesses—that will bring you success on the river in spite of what is being thrown at you.

Technical Water

What is technical water? I am fortunate to guide people from all over the United States. I hear comments from those folks about how technical a fishery they have heard the South Platte can be. I'm talking specifically of the South Platte from Cheesman Dam down to where it meets up with the North Fork of the South Platte. One nonresident told me that he heard from his hometown fly shop that fishing the South Platte is like going to graduate school for fly fishing. I recently guided a client that I have fished with several times over the years, and he confided that he didn't put a fish in the net for the first two years he fly-fished it!

The South Platte is a typical tailwater, fairly consistent water temperatures, diverse insect populations, sporadic hatches, and a wonderful combination of seams, islands, cutbanks, bars, shelves, eddies, and obstructions. It has everything one would want in a fly fishery. I believe the South Platte can be challenging, but is it more technical that other rivers? If so, why? Let's dig deeper.

I've fished other tailwaters in the Rocky Mountain West and have found that, yes, some fish easier than others. Most have many of the same characteristics of the South Platte but seem to give up fish a bit easier. Most of these tailwaters sported the same species of fish, roughly the same insect diversity, and fairly comparable fish numbers. By comparison, most freestones I've fished through my career are typically easier to solve, so I will leave freestone rivers out of this discussion.

Knowing how I define a technical fishery, I decided to put the question to various people. Most, when asked, replied that a technical fishery requires small insects, fine tippets, and stealth. Other replies centered around year-round fishing and recreational pressure, and the fact that most technical rivers are tailwaters. I agree to a point.

I agree with the notion that technical fisheries have all of the above, but I disagree that you can only fish them with certain gear and tackle combinations. In other words, I see all rivers as technical to varying degrees. Some simply require a bit more technique. That's why I prefer to call technical waters "technique waters" instead. One doesn't have to throw size 24 midges on 7X tippet to be successful on the South Platte; one just has to apply the proper techniques.

Now, if you can consistently catch fish on the South Platte, then I believe you can catch fish pretty much anywhere. You have to take your skills and techniques to the next level to consistently catch fish. For most of the year, I and most guides I know, rig with 5X tippets, run bugs that match the naturals' sizes, and fish right through the heavily pressured times. We realize that throwing tiny bugs won't overcome less than desirable drift mechanics, and 7X tippet doesn't reduce drag. Throw bugs that match the hatch, throw them well and in the right spots, and you will hook fish.

Tom Uba preparing to fly-fish technique water.

On this particular technique water, you won't find a bunch of 7- to 8-inch fish. Most of the fish are larger, experience less competition, will eat selectively, and display what appears to be experience. The fish are harder to fool without a doubt, but if they are fished properly, they will eat.

Familiarity breeds success. I remember the first couple of times I fished Cheesman Canyon. I was stunned by how much technique was required to fool those fish. The more I fished it, the more it began to give up fish. My technique remained the same, but I learned a bit each time out, and with success came confidence. Then I started to guide it, and that gave me a brand-new perspective. Fly-fishing the same water with others' gear and skill levels really makes you refine techniques.

Success requires more than just knowing where fish hold and why they are there; it's about overcoming all trout defenses, as you apply everything you have in your arsenal. From knot tying to fly selection and drift mechanics, your technique is critical to your success. It's the fortitude to keep working on your skills and gaining experience that will begin to pay dividends. That's why I guide several clients a year who, after a few days fishing solo and getting their teeth kicked in, hire a guide for half a day to crack the code. It flattens out the learning curve markedly.

To catch fish while nymphing on any river requires knowledge and skill in applying the drift mechanics of depth, speed, profile, and color. When fishing technique water, you have to be able to put all of the mechanics together so they operate as one. I've fished less difficult technique water and noticed that I can get away without having to dial in exact depth, or maybe I can get away with less than perfect speed or a bit more drag in the drift. The river still has all the physical characteristics of the South Platte, but for various reasons the fish behave differently. Don't be fooled into thinking I am referring to waters that produce a bunch of smaller fish. On the contrary, I have fished several less technical waters that produce larger fish.

It doesn't really matter why the fish behave differently in one river compared to the next, why one river is technical and the next is not. What it boils down to is what skills and knowledge you employ to overcome the difficulties presented. Once you are able to apply techniques to catch fish in tougher technique waters, with a little familiarity you can catch fish in any river.

Xs and Os

- Learn to monitor how the water temperatures, water clarity, water flows, and the weather that can affect fishing. Journal it!
- Develop options to overcome a fish's defense.
- Learn to fish technique waters.

5

Reading Water and Fish

Spending many days guiding on the South Platte River below Deckers, Colorado, I know that river pretty well. Because of the decomposed granite that covers the bottom from the erosion caused by the Hayman fire, the river bottom changes daily. Add this fact to the constant bumps and drops in flow from water usage and seasonal flows, and you have a river that changes its personality frequently. The South Platte is getting better yearly with insect numbers, water quality, and trout recruitment, but we still have to contend with the changes. Shelves, bars, and runs that were here today can be gone tomorrow, so the ability to understand what fish need to survive, linked to a good understanding of how to read the water, is critical if you want to consistently put fish in the net.

Typical Run

Reading the water tells you where fish may be holding and why. A typical run consists of a riffle that flows to a pool that empties into a tailout. Some folks call the section between a riffle and the pool a run, but for simplicity, I call the entire section a run and break it into the three parts: riffle, pool, tailout. A typical run can be any length but starts with a riffle and ends when the tailout meets another riffle.

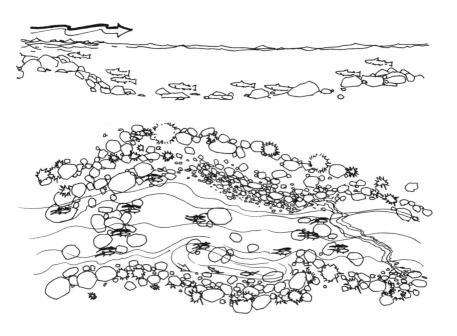

Always strive to locate the riffle, pool, and tailout of runs.

It can be intimidating to walk up to a river, especially some of the bigger ones, and attempt to read the water. I read many years ago in a book by Bill Edrington (*Fly Fishing the Arkansas: An Angler's Guide and Journal*) to dissect a river into three longitudinal parts: left, center, and right. That is great advice because it allows you to find typical runs in each section. Once you learn to identify runs and their specific parts, you can then begin to systematically identify where trout hold and why.

Riffles

A riffle can be as wide as the river or encompass only one longitudinal section. Riffles are deep enough to hold fish, are well oxygenated, and are usually shallower than other parts of a run. On the San Juan River in New Mexico, I've seen trout hold in riffles with their dorsal fins protruding out of the water. Riffle bottoms are typically flatter than other sections and have fewer obstructions, but other objects, such as boulders, can add pockets to a riffle. Because fish are typically exposed to predation and constant current in riffles, they move into them for basically two reasons: to eat and to spawn.

A riffle usually flows over a shelf as it empties into a pool. Keep this in mind as we get into how to fish a typical run. Riffle fish, or as Jeremy Hyatt of Flies and Lies refers to them, sand fish, don't have the luxury of being able to closely inspect flies as they drift by quickly. Couple that advantage with the reason why fish are in the riffle in the first place, and you have a good chance of catching fish in these holds.

Pools

As the riffle flows over the shelf, it deposits in the pool section of the run. Pools are slower and deeper than riffles, and the surface of the water is generally flatter. Some folks call this section a glide, slick, or mirror water. Don't be fooled; some pools have fairly turbulent surface water from gradient structure. To locate the pool section, look for the discernable spot where the riffle ends. This is easy to locate because the riffle water begins to deepen and fall into the head of the pool, usually over a shelf. Water temperatures in a pool are cooler than most water in a river because of water depth, and pools make great havens for fish to hold in the heat of the day; however, many fish like to cruise up into riffles sometimes when the sky is high and air and water temperature rise. They do this for a couple different reasons: one, they are bumped out of typical holds from fishing pressure; two, the cool, oxygenated rif- fle water is a great hold during the heat of the day; and three, they are there to eat or spawn. Not a bad idea to scour those areas when those conditions are present. The head of the pool is fairly well oxygenated because it reaps the benefits of the oxygen-laced riffle water, and fish move into this area readily to feed. Below the head of the pool, or the area where the shelf is formed, is the midpool section.

The midpool is typically the slowest and deepest section of the pool. It holds fish, and like all sections of the river, there is a reason they are there. The fish in this section, depending on flows, temperatures, and oxygenation, may be willing to eat but probably won't be opportunistic feeders, since flies drift by at slower speeds, giving fish a good chance to selectively inspect them. Also, because of slower flows, fish in the midpool for the most part have to move to eat. I usually work these fish a few times before moving up to the shelf area.

The next section downstream is what I refer to as the lower pool. This is usually a secure lie, where fish aren't feeding. They're often there for other reasons such as resting or recuperating from being hooked. This section of the pool typically exhibits the slowest and calmest water in the run. The end of the pool is what I call the tailout section.

Tailout

The tailout is where the water begins to become shallower and move at a faster clip. On the downstream side of a typical lower pool you will find an incline on the bottom that prepares the way for another set of riffles. This section holds fish, and if conditions are right, you can pick up dominant fish here. As the water picks up speed, it begins to pick up insects, and if there are good holds for fish, you should pick up a few. Anytime you compress the river horizontally, as in a tailout, you compress the amount of food.

One tailout I fish through regularly forms after a long riffle and a fairly long pool. As the pool begins to tail out, a line of rocks creates the beginning of the next riffle. Some of the best fish in the river reside there, and they eat if you can sneak up and a get a good presentation to them. I prefer to fish this section in the afternoon, after several fly fishers have been through, because piles of fish have been moved into this tailout. Most people walk right by this section without fishing it because some tailouts, like this one, are fairly inconspicuous.

Usually, but not as a constant rule, if the day is cloudy, or it is near dusk or dawn, fish will feel safe enough to move out into feeding lanes in the tailout section to eat. Likewise, if a fish moves up into the midpool or up to the shelf upstream through the pool, it's game on. They are looking to eat. There is no discernible rule about how long or short a run can be. It is what it is, so learn to look for observable clues to help you locate where one section melts into another.

Bends, Eddies, Confluences, and Islands

Once you have a good handle on locating a typical run, you can begin to use that information to help you locate fish throughout the entire river. I like a river that is diverse, one that has several characteristics such as bends, eddies, and islands. The more diverse the characteristics, the easier it is to read the water and locate fish. The Middle Fork of the South Platte is such a river. It has a series of short runs between tight bends that fish amazingly alike. A river like that is a great place to hone your water reading skills.

The key to fly-fishing a diverse river, or any river, is to identify where two or more seams converge, where seams are forced to one side of the river, or where undercuts, foam lines, or backeddies exist.

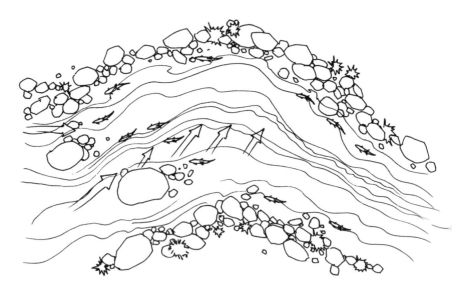

Notice how the seams converge to create a food "super highway," and how in a bend, the insects and seams are forced to one side

Remember, you're looking for typical run characteristics amid diverse river characteristics. Simply put, look for the areas where trout have to inhabit to thrive or survive. Like my friend John Axelson says, "If it looks fishy, it is fishy, so fish the fishy spots." Learn to locate the fishy spots.

Pocketwater

Years ago, I arrived early at the fly shop to meet my clients. As we were making sure the paperwork was filled out, one of them asked me where we were planning to fish. I told her where I planned to take them, and they both shuffled their feet and said that they wanted to fish the Blue River at spot X, to which I replied, "Sure, no problem." Little did they know, I had never stepped a wading boot in that river section. I was nervous on the drive up and over the Continental Divide, as I attempted to call other guides that had been on that stretch. Finally I got a hold of

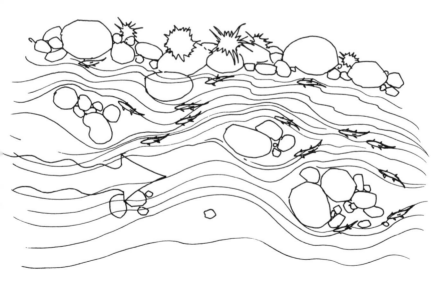

Notice the U- or horseshoe-shaped seams that pockets create. Don't forget to fish the front of the pocket as well.

one guide, and he told me to hang a right when I cross the bridge out of town. "Park there, and fish your way up," was his advice. As we crossed the bridge where I needed to turn, I caught a glimpse of the river we were going to fish, and my spirits jumped. Pocketwater! Oh baby, life is good!

Pocketwater is just that, a pocket or a place for fish to hold. A pocket is formed below an obstruction, like a protruding rock. Pockets are basically comprised of a seam, a pocket, and another seam.

You might run into many pockets in a run or just a few. A series of pockets that connect together can make up an entire run, as was the case on the section of the Blue where I guided that day.

The reason that I was overjoyed to see pocketwater is that I have a systematic approach to fishing it. Two seams from adjoining pockets can make a small confluence that eventually becomes a seam for another pocket. Imagine adding two conveyor belts of food into one slot. If you see two or more seams coming together as one, you will find fish. Locating fish in pocketwater can be simple because the seams act as conveyors for food and the pockets hold fish that feel safe and are likely to eat opportunistically. Pocketwater is your friend.

Fish Needs

Now that we have a common terminology for breaking down a river, let's examine why fish hold where they do. Just like those who pursue them, fish need three things: food, oxygen, and shelter. The places where fish hold in a river, in an attempt to provide for those needs, are called lies. There are different types of lies that folks describe with different names. I refer to the basic lies as prime, secondary, and safe or secure. Prime lies are the fish lies that supply food, oxygen, and shelter the best.

You'll typically see dominant fish holding in these spots because of characteristics of the currents, the amount of food and oxygen, and safety from shelter that's only a fin flip away. In other words, this fish not only has its needs met, but it doesn't have to work hard for a meal. It's not unusual to see a dominant fish chasing off subordinate intruders to protect his spot. I have often seen dominant fish caught off of their lie, only to witness a subordinate fish set up shop in that spot immediately.

Secondary lies usually hold subordinate fish. With conditions being equal, these are good lies but usually don't provide the higher quality shelter, food, or ease and comfort in gathering a meal that the prime lies offer. I fish the heck out of secondary lies; I would imagine that's where most fish are caught. There are only so many prime lies in a river.

Behind secondary lies are what I call safe or secure lies. I call fish in secure lies "belly fish." Belly fish are laying back in the runs usually in the lower pool and are basically not interested in eating at this time, but they feel safe where they are stationed. I've witnessed fish that we have just landed and released as they mope down to secure lies to rest. It's not unusual to see them move back into secondary lies after a brief period of time, when they will begin to eat again.

Knowing the differences between lies helps us understand why fish want one lie over another, why dominant fish set up where they do, and how subordinate fish react to openings in the lie hierarchy. It's all about

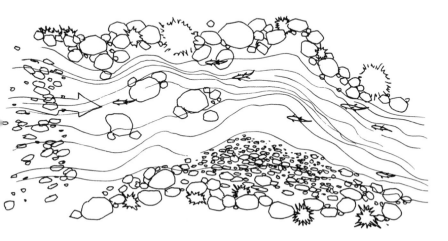

Prime lies supply the best food, oxygen, and shelter. Secondary lies usually hold subordinate fish, and safe lies are secure.

competition between fish. I'll explain this phenomenon with an example from my own experience.

Jeremy Hyatt and I have often guided larger groups together. We have seen the competition between fish in a single run on several occasions, and until recently we didn't quite put the entire picture together. In one particular run, there's a riffle bend that bounces off a rock wall, filters onto a short shelf, and finally flows into a long pool section consisting of a sandy bottom.

As we enter this section, we always see a few fish in the pool. Our clients can always pick a fish off of the sandy bottom of this pool because of its proximity to the short shelf. We pick up one or two fish out of the pool and begin to spread folks out. After spreading clients out on the tailout, shelf, and riffle, we watch a phenomenon occur. The first and last handful of fish we catch are always the largest and most dominant in the run.

Because the first fish are the larger, dominant fish, they get the first crack at the bugs. The next group of fish we catch are the subordinate fish on secondary lies, and in this section subordinate fish fill the voids left by previously hooked fish almost immediately. The last group of fish we pick off are again larger, dominant fish because we stuck to our system and fished our way up and into the run. In other words, we are hitting the best lies on the far side of the run last, thus picking off fish that evacuated the main run during all the fun we had fishing the main body.

Here's another interesting tidbit: as we hooked, landed, and released fish, the pool section began to fill with recently hooked, pouting fish. Hooked fish most often cruise to safe holding water to recuperate. We don't fish to those fish, even though you can see them begin to tentatively feed again. Most of the time, we enter that run with a couple fish in the pool and leave with several holding in it. It's a great little gem, and we are very careful with it.

Clients ask me all the time, "How did you spot that fish?" I explain that the best way to start spotting fish, aside from good eyewear, is to know where they are likely to hold. Once you figure out *where* they are, you can then start to read the fish and realize *why* they are there. Once you discern where and why fish hold in portions of a run, you can begin to move to the next step, which is to formulate a game plan to catch them. This game plan is a huge component of your playbook and should be complete and well thought out.

Xs and Os

- Learn to recognize the elements of a typical run.
- Learn to locate where seams converge.
- Identify eddies, bars, seams, pockets, undercuts, and other river characteristics.
- Understand basic fish needs and how those needs affect where fish live in a river.
- Identify prime, secondary, and safe or secure lies.
- Learn how to spot fish based on their needs, reading the water, and typical fish lies.

6

The Drift Draft

Now that you have the basis for your nymph rig and the versatility and foundation it gives you, it's time to progress to the next page in your playbook. It's time to draft some skilled players to complement the rig. The way you rig up is the constant, or static, and the adjustments to the rig are dynamic. In this year's draft we are going to select Depth, Speed, Profile, and Color. All fantastic players in their own right, but when you combine them with the foundation you've established, you create a formidable offense. The better you control these four factors, the better you will nymph-fish. It's that simple. We will break down these four factors, and then apply what we discussed to the entire package of the drift in the following chapter.

Depth

Attaining and maintaining the proper depth throughout the drift is critical; therefore, the ability to quickly change drift depth is imperative. Let's look at a typical pocketwater scenario. To recap, the body of water consists of a seam, a pocket, and a seam. Basically, it's horseshoe shaped and has three different characteristics of drift. Your goal is to fish the pocket correctly, breaking it down into three different parts. If you fish each part the same, then you're not fishing it correctly. The inside seam may be a different depth and speed than the outside seam, and the pocket will most definitely be different from the seams. Microadjustments to depth can make a big difference in helping put your flies into the columns where the fish are holding.

When you move into a section of the run, you need to estimate water depth and adjust your depth accordingly. Again, to test yourself and see if you're reading the depth properly, you can always step into what you've already fished to test your estimating skills. You're probably thinking that you have to move the indicator for each scenario, but that doesn't always hold true. Advanced nymph fishers have figured out how to attack varied water and pocket scenarios with a base nymph rig and subtle changes in casting angles to accommodate water speeds and depth.

While beginning and intermediate anglers should stay as consistent as possible with short line drifts, the advanced angler can basically use the same rig, make microadjustments, and fish pocketwater effectively. You are striving to fish different types of water without having to constantly move your indicator up or down. If you have set up the initial base rig correctly, having close to the proper depth and weight from the get-go, you can effectively nymph any water using angles, casting distances, and slight depth adjustments. I'll dig into this in depth a bit later.

I have never seen a fish move down in the water column to take a fly. I'm fairly sure someone has, but I haven't. Because of the way their eyes are placed on their heads, fish have difficulty seeing below them under their mouth. I believe this is why they typically feed at the level they are in or above. That's why, when I guide or fish and I am not seeing fish, or I'm blind-nymphing runs, I start at the bottom of the water column and work my way up. Starting at the lowest level and working your way up through the columns is more efficient than trying to work down to the fish. If I try to work down to the fish that I don't see, it may take me several adjustments to get to the level I need to drift, and the disruption may spook or put the fish off feeding patterns. If I see fish, or I am sight-nymphing, I start at the fish's level in the column or slightly above. I go into great detail about sight-nymphing later.

If you're blind-nymphing and you're not ticking the bottom regularly, you're not deep enough. It's not the weight we are concerned with here, it's the length of line under the indicator. Remember, the formula for depth is $1^{1}/_{2}$ times the depth of the water you are fishing, and you should use the reality rule to ensure you're where you need to be.

Speed

It's not unusual for a rookie quarterback, straight out of college, to struggle early on in his career. You hear coaches and coordinators talking about how he will become more effective as the game slows down. You have to slow down your nymphing as well. Provided you are mending properly, you should put on enough weight so that your indicator travels roughly half the speed of the water surface. Why half the speed? The water surface is traveling roughly half the speed of the water at grade under your boots.

Because of differences in substrates, this formula is simply a rule of thumb, but suffice it to say the surface water is running faster than the water at your feet. Any fly fisher who has spent more than a few days standing in current realizes there's a lot going on subsurface. Obstructions, gravel and rock size and shape, streambed angles and gradients, and even air resistance on the water surface all factor into the equation. If you make sure your indicator travels the speed of the water surface, thinking you are getting a dead drift, your flies are actually traveling about twice as fast as the speed at grade. You may pick up a fish here or there, but you are certainly missing out on the majority of fish.

It's easy to pick out a bubble, stick, leaf, or something else to measure the speed of your indicator. Your indicator should be cruising half the speed of the other object as you compare the two during the drift. Add weight to slow down the drift; remove weight to speed it up. Depending on water flows, I usually start with a BB-size split shot in heavier water and a size 6 split shot in lighter water.

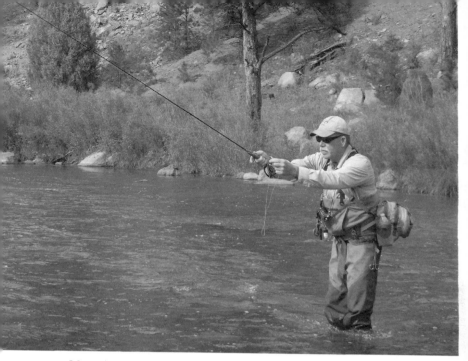

Measuring the speed of your indicator is simple and observable.

When you're not achieving the speed you need, you can add or subtract weight as needed. I like to use tungsten putty to micromanage drift speed. Simply pinch some on above the split shot, and dip it in the water to set it before you cast. Once you get to a point that you are beginning to have a large amount of putty on the weight, it's time to pinch some off and add another split shot.

Adding weight is not a method for controlling depth as much as controlling speeds, although weight can help you get your flies down faster in the drift. Increased weight adds additional drag, which slows the drift. I always tell clients that depth is depth, and weight is speed. A drift that matches the water speed without drag is a dead drift. Through experience and trial and error, you will be able to estimate how much weight to apply before you hit the river; however, you will always have to micromanage it.

Speed kills. If you have the right depth, but the wrong speed, your chances of hooking fish decline markedly. If you have the proper speed at the wrong depth, at least you have a chance to pick up fish in that particular water column. Getting the two to play as a unit is incredibly important.

Proper speed and depth is deadly on both opportunistic and selectively feeding fish. As a matter of fact, I will adjust my depth and speed several times before I even consider changing my bugs. If you have those two dialed in, but are throwing the wrong flies, you still have a chance to pick up fish. If you have the perfect flies, and don't fish proper depth and speed, you're in for a long day.

Profile and Color

When I talk of profile, I am talking about how your chosen fly appears to fish in their environment. It's important to have the proper profile, and that includes the size and stage of the fly, that matches what the fish are eating. I will devote some time to entomology later, but profile, linked to depth and speed, is the Xs and Os of the nymph drift. Dial in depth, speed, and profile, and you're cooking with gas.

Opportunistic fish eat a wide variety of food, move side to side and up in the water column to track something down, and are generally fun to fish. Selectively feeding fish are as equally fun to fish but can be more of a challenge because they may be eating one stage of one particular bug, in only one slot, and in only one column. You can get away with a slightly faulty rig and still catch opportunistically feeding fish. To consistently hook selectively feeding fish, you've got to have things dialed in. A slight mistake in profile, if depth and speed are good, can make the difference in how many you can catch in technique water.

I am amazed but not amused when I run into selectively feeding fish. I had an old guide friend of mine explain that "fish ain't intelligent; they're just really focused!" Fish seem intelligent when they won't eat a great offering. In fact they're usually just being selective.

So let's say depth, speed, and profile are solid, but I still can't catch that selective-feeding, presumably vegetarian trout. I know it's eating because I can see it swing side to side in the column. I know I've put my bugs by that fish, but I keep getting prom date refusals. Can it be I have to go deeper into the playbook? Is the color of the fly going to make a difference? When you are certain that everything else is dialed in, including size and stage of fly, and you continue to have selective feeding fish snub your offering, it's time to consider changing the color of your fly. Whether you're not catching fish because of weather conditions, water clarity, seasonal hatches, or fly fatigue, if you are certain that your rig is close to perfect, and you're not catching fish, finally look at changing fly color.

Sometimes a subtle change in fly color can elicit a strike. Recently, I was guiding during a day that the fish were being particularly selective. I was running a size 18 black Copper John under a San Juan Worm. Fish would swing on our bugs, but they would not eat. I was confident in our rig, so I changed the black Copper John to a red one in the same size. Dang, that's all it took. Black and red must look somewhat similar to fish underwater, and the color contrast must have made the difference. The fish ate so well that we even went back and fished runs we hit previously. They ain't smart, just focused!

By now I'm sure you've noticed that one skill set leads into and is the basis for the next skill set. As a former teacher and coach, I've seen how important it is to build individual players using this method. At this point you should have a working knowledge of the basic nymph rig and know how important depth, speed, profile, and color are. You should be able to see how this all meshes together. Now it's time to move on to the meat and potatoes of nymphing: the drift.

Xs and Os

- Learn to estimate water depth and to set your rig depth quickly and efficiently.
- Practice slowing the game down by using weight to adjust for proper drift speed.
- Understand opportunistic and selective feeding fish.
- Know how fly profile and color factor into the drift.
- Remember this order: Depth, Speed, Profile, Color.

7

Nymphing the Drift

I always tell my clients, "Don't let your fly line come between you and a good drift." A perfect drift would present your flies drag-free, at the correct depth and speed, with the proper profile and color of the nymph the fish are eating. How you do this is a function of setting up the proper rig for nymphing and employing what you know about depth, speed, profile, and color. Couple this with solid drift fundamentals and techniques, and you're well on your way. It sounds like a daunting task, but when you learn the fundamentals of the drift, it will all come together. The main idea of mending is to remember that you have to mend the line that you can't pick off the water. In other words, the more line you can take off the water through managing your slack, the less line you have to mend. The goal is to present a dead drift that appears completely natural, and the method to achieve that goal is line and fly rod control and mending.

Mending

In order to prevent drag, which causes an unnatural presentation of your nymphs, it is imperative that you learn to mend both horizontally *and* vertically. For advanced anglers, I am confident you can mend horizontally; however, the vertical mend is just as important and often overlooked. I prefer to short-line nymph, using 8 to 10 feet of fly line and implementing short, drag-free drifts. Sometimes you have to extend your nymphing range and use long-line nymphing. If push comes to shove, I'd still rather move my feet closer to the quarry than long-line nymph. Short-line nymphing is much more efficient.

The shorter the line, the more time you have to set the hook when a fish eats. The more line you have snaking to the indicator, the quicker you have to be on the set. It's common knowledge that fish eat and spit all day; what's not so common knowledge is the speed at which they can spit your offering. Shorter distances equate to quicker sets; quicker sets equal more hookups.

Horizontal drag is something you can see and fix easily. Usually, a quick glance will clue you in to drag from the fly line being pulled one way or another during the drift. You will notice wakes formed by your indicator as it's zipping along on the surface faster than the water is traveling, or you will see the indicator being pulled out of the original longitudinal plane that you initially placed it in.

In the illustration on the next page, notice the huge belly formed downstream (right to left flow) of the indicator that will essentially

Nymphing with a flat fly rod, a short mended line, a management loop, and the rod tip pointing at the indicator provides for a solid drift and a quick hook set.

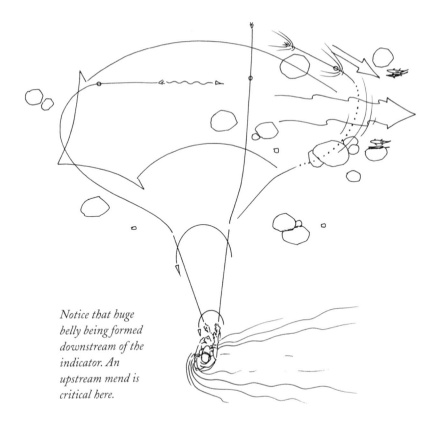

Notice that huge belly being formed downstream of the indicator. An upstream mend is critical here.

move your bugs too fast and pull you out of the path you intended to fish. The belly would be easy to fix by taking up the line slack and drawing a small circle around the indicator in the upstream (right) direction.

Again, you can only mend what you can take off the water. Too often, I watch anglers try to long-line mend without taking up the slack first. Simply pull in some slack with the management loop, point your fly rod directly at the indicator, and draw a small circle in the direction you wish to mend. The illustration on the previous page shows an example of mending all the way to the indicator using the management loop with a flat fly rod. The key is to prepare for the mend by taking up all slack using the management loop. Mending is all about give and take, and the management loop is key in doing this properly.

Short-line nymphing and high sticking put the angler right over the indicator. When you high-stick, you should only have a couple feet of monofilament on the water throughout the drift. Short-line nymphing, as I see it, is when you have less than 15 feet of fly line on the water. After the initial cast, usually a 45-degree angle upstream, you immediately adjust the slack out of the presentation while flattening out the fly rod using the management loop.

The management loop is a critical component of a good drift because you can use it to add or remove line from the drift. I notice a lot of anglers who like to hold the loop in their off-rod hand. Instead of that method, I like to teach folks to loosely pinch the fly line under their index finger with their rod hand, while holding the management loop with the other hand. In this way, you can manage the loop best and can quickly add or subtract line while being ready to set at any instant by simply pinching the fly line to the rod handle cork.

One thing I do to keep my clients honest and not fish too much line is to only allow them to add to the drift the amount of fly line in their management loop. Usually, the management loop is a loop of about 36 inches behind their rod handle. As they drift, they can add up to the loop amount to the overall drift length. Adding management

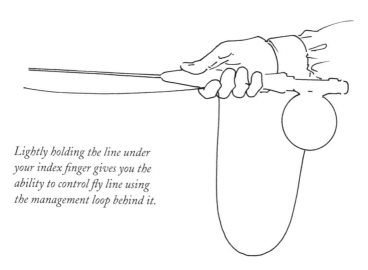

Lightly holding the line under your index finger gives you the ability to control fly line using the management loop behind it.

loop line to the drift rarely extends the drift, it is actually a tool used to perfect the drift. Perfect drifts are usually short drifts.

Adding any more line than the management loop to the drift is not only ineffective, but it can be detrimental. I call this "out-casting your coverage." It's similar to a punter kicking the ball so far that his coverage team can't effectively cover the kick. The same holds true for the nymph drift; you get so much line in play you can't possibly manage it all. When you out-cast your coverage, *you* become the fulcrum or the pivot point of the drift and you can't fish horizontal seams properly. You have to uncomfortably attempt to mend way too much line, and the tempo of the entire drift is ruined. This pulls you out of the seams you're trying to fish.

How do you know you're out-casting your coverage? You will rarely get a drag-free drift that stays in the same horizontal seam or plane you put it in, you will be uncomfortable trying to keep up with mending, and quite frankly you won't be catching as many fish as the guy next to you. All of this will be further defined in subsequent chapters.

A flat fly rod, whether you are short-line or long-line nymphing, is critical because it allows you to keep the indicator and flies in the desired plane. If your fly rod is at any angle greater than parallel to the water, you will inadvertently cause the drift to take an arc-shaped path, pulling your flies out of the intended seam.

I've watched countless anglers fish dry flies over the years, and I can't recall ever seeing a dry-fly fisher ever use anything but a flat fly rod. It's just more conducive to achieving a solid drift. Why then would you fly fish nymphs with anything but a flat fly rod? A fly rod fished with the rod tip higher than the reel causes dreaded drag and shortens your drift through the feeding zone dramatically because *you* become a fulcrum as your bugs are pulled away from the intended drift path or plane.

To defeat drag, and that's the main goal in your dead drift, your flat fly rod must be pointed directly at your indicator throughout all stages of the drift and you must manage your line well with mending techniques. I often have to battle to overcome incomplete mending with clients by adding much more weight than what's called for. As

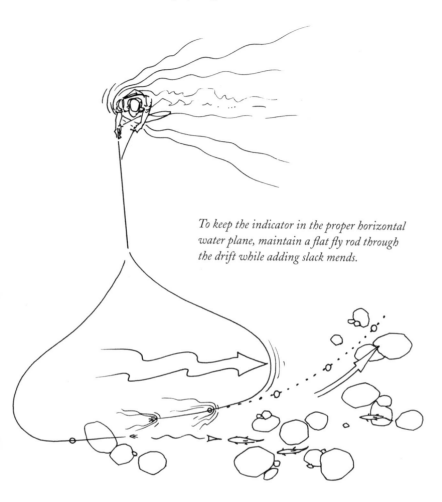

To keep the indicator in the proper horizontal water plane, maintain a flat fly rod through the drift while adding slack mends.

they begin to manage the drift better, weight begins to disappear. It's like a diet.

Mending upstream is counterintuitive. The river is flowing in one direction, and most times you are mending in the other. I notice a bunch of folks who lose the smooth, continuous qualities of the drift because the drift is going one direction with the current, and a proper mend is often placed in the other direction. Here's a tip for those of you learning to mend and those of you who are teaching buddies or

Alan Peak with a complete mend.

clients to mend: begin by completing several high-stick drifts without adding a mend. Stress the importance of having the flat fly rod tip travel at the speed of the indicator. Point the rod tip right at the indicator. Also, focus on the connection between the fly rod speed and the water speed. Take the fly rod out of the rod hand and practice moving the fly rod hand at the speed of the water while you point to where the indicator should be in the drift.

After several drifts you should have a good tempo and perfect rod-hand speed. At this point in the exercise, add an imaginary mend to the drift by simply drawing a circle the opposite direction of the drift. Make the circle about 6 inches in diameter. Draw a flat line left to right at the speed of the water, and then draw a circle upstream or counterclockwise as you continue a smooth drift with your hand. Do this several times as you begin to add several upstream circles to the imaginary drift. What you will find is that, in short order, you can quickly follow and continue a smooth drift while upstream mending. If you begin to struggle a bit, simply put the rod down and get some practice in.

Another common problem beginner and intermediate fly fishers make is that they constantly want to put out more fly line. This just accentuates problems because it's hard enough to manage 10 feet of line, let alone 20. It is not only inefficient, and hard to set with a bunch of line out, but it is nearly impossible to keep a drag-free presentation with 15 to 20 feet of fly line below you. If you want to fish the area that far below you, then you should move your feet to where you can fish it effectively.

One tip you may want to employ, if you don't already do it, is to use a two-handed method of mending. When I teach folks to mend, I tell them they should be able to mend without having to take their eyes off of the indicator. How many times have you had a fish eat in the middle of a mend? That happens often, and you can multiply the misses by taking your eyes off of the indicator because you are mending. Missing

The ability to mend without taking your eyes off of the indicator is crucial. The "off-rod" hand seamlessly moves to the rod hand.

a fish that eats during a mend you can accept, but missing a fish because you didn't even know it ate is taboo.

The rod hand and loop hand should work in unison. The line under your trigger finger on your rod hand should be held loosely to allow for mending slack to the drift, and for sucking up line from the drift. Usually, the only time you pinch cork is on a set or the cast. As you prepare to mend, you need to have the management loop line in the fingers of your loop hand. You should control the 36-inch management loop at about the center or bottom of the loop. Simply pull up the slack in the drift to prepare for the mend, and with a flat fly rod, draw a small circle in the direction you wish to mend while adding slack to the mend.

Here's the kicker: as you add slack line to the mend, your line hand should move toward and touch your rod hand. In this way you can keep your head up, and you will only add a measured amount of slack to the drift. Once you begin to employ the two-handed method, you will find it much more enjoyable to fish with your head up as you control line coming in and going out during the drift.

The more line you have on the water, the harder managing the drift becomes, and the quicker you have to be with your set. It's just plain inefficient. Concentrate on keeping things as short and simple as possible while you focus on the keys to a good drift. Mending plays a huge part of this.

Keys to a Good Drift

The main concept of mending is to arrange your fly line in such a way as to provide for various currents. Here are some keys to a good mend.

- Learn to recognize when your drift is under drag. Watch your indicator to see if it is creating wakes, moving faster than the water, or pulling out of the desired horizontal drift plane.
- Take up your slack line using your management loop. You can only mend what you can take off the water!
- Strive to mend far to near all the way to the indicator first. It's good practice to mend to the indicator first, and then mend progressively

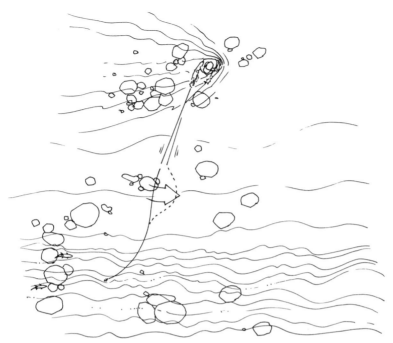

A hinge will occur where water speeds differ. If you can't high-stick it, micro-mend at seams. Remember, your first mend is usually all the way to the indicator, then you micro-mend hinges that form during the drift.

closer using micromends. By the way, a micromend, as I refer to it, is designed to mend only sections of your line that are being hinged by current. This method is bulletproof and will help overcome those drifts that have several seams that cause line hinges. Hinges form in water seams that have differing speeds. Even though your initial mend is all the way to the indicator, because of water speed differences you usually have to employ micromends to hinges.

- Point your flat fly rod at your indicator throughout the drift. This puts you in position to efficiently and quickly mend to the indicator or to hinges and set quickly.
- With your flat fly rod pointing at your indicator, and all slack picked up, draw a small circle around your indicator in the direction you wish to mend.

- Develop the ability to flawlessly mend in one direction while continuing to follow the indicator with your rod tip. Sounds easier than it is. It's counterintuitive to mend upstream, all the way to the indicator, while keeping your fly rod moving the opposite direction. It takes practice.
- Learn to mend while adding slack. This will help keep you in the plane you wish the indicator to travel in. Again, I don't think it's advantageous to keep stripping out line in an attempt to lengthen your drift. Try to use only your management loop to mend.
- Learn to pick up and place your line behind your indicator while short-line nymphing. It's as easy as it sounds; simply pick up your fly line and leader and place it upstream or downstream of your indicator.
- Learn to mend vertically using a pause mend. Remember, there are vertical differences in water velocity through the water columns.
- Learn to mend your line by using various casts, such as the reach mend and the roll/reach mend (see chapter 11).

Stages of the Drift

I break the drift into three simple stages: the initial, the middle, and the swing stage. If you are blind-nymphing where you can't see your flies or fish, you have to be able to see what your bugs are doing in your mind's eye. Practice and experience will help you develop this skill. The ability to visualize where your flies are when you can't see them is important because you will learn to mend what you can't see. Trust me, once you get good at this, you will begin to anticipate when the strike will occur. Just keep mending horizontally and vertically, and as you begin to hook fish, you'll begin to see underwater. It's tough to explain, but it's like when you throw a ball and you know the instant it leaves your hand that it's going to hit the target. Your brain takes over.

The initial stage occurs the instant your bugs hit the water. You want to keep the rod tip low initially, flatten out your fly rod, and pick up any slack as soon as possible. This will get your bugs into the zone

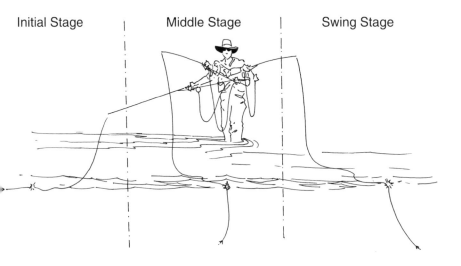

| Initial Stage | Middle Stage | Swing Stage |

Each drift stage is critical to the entire drift.

quickly. This is especially effective as you fish a riffle that drops to a shelf. Fish like to hold there, and you want your bugs in the right spot as soon as possible.

A lot of folks are complacent at this stage, thinking the action comes later in the drift. This couldn't be further from the truth, and if you use the proper technique, you can pick up several fish in the initial stage. I'm not sure why exactly, but a lot of folks I guide have a habit of throwing an upstream mend into the drift as soon as the line hits the water. This will pull you right out of the horizontal plane you cast to and pull your bugs up in the column, thus rendering the initial stage less useful. It is a bad habit to get into.

I realize that there are instances that you must mend as soon as your flies hit the water; however you can do a couple of things to improve the initial stage and the remainder of the drift. If you consistently pull the bugs up into the columns at the initial stage, you may never get the bugs where you want them in the last two stages of the drift. To avoid this, learn a reach mend and add it to your cast. It's simple and effective. Another way to prevent drift damage is to learn to mend with a high, flat stick. Simply suck in fly line using a flat fly rod and the management loop. Mend the line back into the drift in the middle stage, and you have provided good drift mechanics. Again, mend only as much slack that is in your management loop, about three feet, and resist the urge to feed additional line.

As you near the middle stage, your flies should be at the intended depth. One way to discern if your flies are getting down quickly enough is to observe when your indicator turns over. Your indicator turns over when your flies and weight are at or near maximum depth. You can usually see the indicator slightly rotate vertically as everything straightens out below it. Watching how fast your indicator moves *when* it turns over in your drift, and you will get a good idea if you are getting the desired depth-to-speed ratio. Your indicator should turn over just as it exits the initial stage. Your flat fly rod should be at its highest elevation above the water.

In most cases, mid-drift is the perfect place to mend a bit of slack to the drift if the water characteristics call for it. If the seam is moving away from you slightly or if you feel the need to slow your drift and add a vertical mend, now's the time to add the slack from the management loop. Don't get greedy; stay disciplined and add a small amount of slack, and watch what happens to the drift characteristics. You should see the indicator melt into the proper speed for a great drift. Again, this isn't about drift length, but drift perfection.

As for the slack mend, simply allow slack to pass through your fingers as you mend behind the indicator. I coach folks to hold the loop with their off hand, and as they add slack to bring their off hand up to their rod hand as they release line. Using this method I've found that I can control the amount of slack released, and by touching my hands together I never have to take my eyes off the indicator. If you look at the illustration of two-hand mending, you'll notice my rod hand index finger releases the line for a slack mend.

As with all of the stages, look for any fish movement in the vicinity of your indicator. What constitutes the vicinity? Well, if you have 5 feet of monofilament under your indicator, look for fish movement (flashes) in at least a 4-foot diameter circle under the indicator. I strive to keep the indicator in view and watch the vicinity at the same time. This skill will greatly enhance your nymphing success and should definitely become part of your playbook. Once you master this skill, you will begin to set on subtle flashes or movements in the vicinity of the indicator. Many times I've watched fish eat the flies, and the indicator doesn't relay the take. You simply miss the fish. However, I rarely see an angler miss a set on a feeding flash.

During the middle stage you look to mend to any vertical as well as horizontal drag. Let's dig back into water column speeds. Water velocities differ substantially from the surface to the grade or bottom because of a few factors we delved into previously. The surface velocity is roughly twice that of the grade, and the middle column is slightly faster than the surface. You can see how the differing speeds can put an arc in your leader and tippet, causing drag on your flies. As the drift nears the middle stage, simply stop your indicator for an instant, gently place your line behind it, and continue your drift. I refer to this as the pause mend,

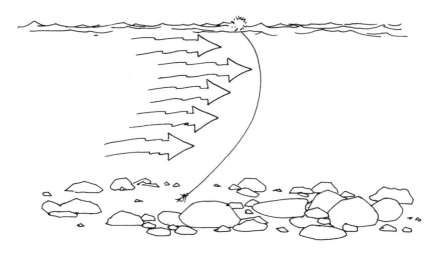

This is a simple example of how water velocity decreases as it nears grade. Clearly, the leader will be affected.

and it takes a bit of practice as you learn to gently stop your indicator, allowing the flies to catch up. You can also do the pause mend while you add slack to your drift—a pause–slack mend combination. It's a fairly advanced skill, but you can master it easily with a bit of practice. Once learned and perfected, it can pay big dividends.

During the last quarter of your middle stage you can throw an additional slack mend or two into the drift if you are adept at nymphing. Again, you need to keep drifts as short as possible. This part of your drift sets you up for your position set or lift techniques that occur in the next drift stage, so you have to ensure that your flies are at full depth before you enter this stage. To achieve full depth, you must mend properly with zero drag. Use the same keys to a good drift as you get near the end of the middle drift stage. Begin to lower your fly rod over the water.

The last and oft overlooked stage is the swing stage. If you do it correctly, you should pick up 20 to 30 percent of your fish here. This is because your bugs are beginning to rise through the water column, which has a tendency to spur fish into eating. They do this partly because they may recognize the nymph during the emergent phase or simply because they think it's getting away. Your fly rod should be low and flat over the water, and your flies will be at least at a 45-degree angle below you. Let your flies begin to rise in the column and employ a position set here.

A position set is nothing more than a short, sweeping action over the water at the end of your drift. Ever skip rocks on a pond? The set is just like that, but in the reverse. Imagine someone videotaped you skipping a rock, and play it backward. That is the position set. You don't want to set too hard, just a quick, fluid motion. Bring your rod tip up as you complete the position set, and finish with your rod hand thumb about as high as your hat brim. Do this religiously; you'll be amazed at how many more fish you'll pick up. Performing the position set properly enhances the drift cadence. It's puts you into a rhythm, slows you down, helps you pay attention to detail, and puts you into position for your roll cast, which we will discuss later.

Upstream vs. Downstream Mends

Unfortunately the water surface is not always uniform enough to allow us to throw in just one mend. In several instances, we must throw in an upstream mend, downstream mend, or both. Most times you can minimize the amount of mending by using short-line high sticking and micromends to the hinges. When a situation calls for it, you can use long-line mending techniques (over 15 feet). Long-line mending usually calls for both upstream and downstream mends to correct for various currents and seams.

Use your upstream mend initially to get the fly line behind or upstream of your indicator, and then add other mends you need to accommodate the various currents. Sometimes you'll run into technical water or long-line drifts that require several upstream or downstream mends to get the drift right. Throw in as many mends as you need, but be careful to take up all the slack you can and check for drag.

Often, when throwing longer nymph casts, you need to add slack to the drift to either get into another seam, stay in a seam that curls away from you, or add slack to set up for a long-line mend to the indicator. You need to build a bigger management loop to accommodate longer casts, and you want a bit extra to pull this mend off. All you are doing is throwing a long, slack S mend into the drift for future use. The technique is fairly easy with a bit of practice and can take your fly fishing to the next level.

In S mending, you throw more slack using a flat fly rod with a down-to-up action. With the fly rod low and flat after the cast, and plenty of loop to borrow from, you simply push the fly rod up and away from yourself while releasing line. Make sure you use enough force to not only get the fly line off the water, but to throw line to the indicator as well. The fly rod usually finishes in a flat plane above your head. Finish this mend off with a side-to-side, snaking motion to build in a shock absorber, of sorts, to the drift. The pictures show the beginning positions and the end positions of the fly rod. It's easier than it looks.

As always check for drag. Vertical drag in long-line nymphing is much tougher to control, because it is difficult to pause-mend all the way to the indicator. You're usually so darn busy managing horizontal line drag during long-line nymphing that a pause mend is not a top priority—or even possible.

Upstream Cast and Presentation

The ability to cast directly upstream and present nymphs is a yet another play you want in your playbook. A few reasons I often use upstream casts are to cover a river along the edges, to work a narrow river that has an abundance of trees lining the banks, or to attack pocketwater. The key to an upstream cast is to present dead-drifted nymphs over fish without lining them.

If you want to fish a seam straight upriver, first look to see if you can change the angle of your cast so the fish sees only your leader and tippet. A simple step left or right can usually give you an angle to accomplish this feat. If you can't move, you can cast and add a reach mend (see page 137) to ensure that your flies are in the fish holding seam but your line is not.

Since your indicator will be coming toward you downriver, you need to employ a different mending technique. Once you finish your cast, resist the urge to pick up your fly rod tip. Leave it right where you stopped the cast, low over the water. Your goal is to keep the indicator moving at the right speed, while taking up the slack that is forming as everything is floating toward you.

With a low, flat fly rod pointing toward your indicator, you manage the drift by managing the fly line directly below your rod tip. The trick here is to strip in enough slack to prevent a loop of fly line from forming on the water below your rod tip, while making sure you're not stripping line too quickly *and* watching your indicator. It's easier than it sounds, and folks I guide pick it up quickly.

If too much line collects on the water under your rod tip, the water will grab it and create drag, making your rig drift too quickly. If you strip line too quickly, you will drag your rig through the run. The loop below the rod tip is the key. It should form roughly a 90-degree angle.

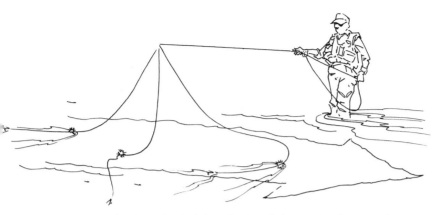

Strive to keep the line loop directly below the fly rod tip at a 90-degree angle to "mend" upstream nymph presentations. The line on the left is mending too fast, causing drag, while the line on the right is mending too slow, also causing drag. The line in the middle is mending correctly. Readers, note the current flowing to the right.

Anything more causes drag; anything less, well, causes more drag. Observe the water around your indicator to see if you have any wakes, and adjust accordingly.

The Almighty Set

Provided you're drifting correctly, the set is a valuable tool for you to learn and implement. A set can occur anytime and anywhere within the drift when your indicator does anything but float naturally. I see a lot of clients who have the bad habit of mending when they should be setting. Instead of setting on anything that looks unnatural, they expect the indicator to suddenly zip underwater with each take. That does happen, but as a matter of fact, most takes are subtle. Sometimes the indicator just pauses slightly, twitches, or rotates.

If you notice that you are missing an inordinate amount of strikes, try decreasing the distance from your indicator to your flies while still maintaining the same drift. If fish are eating, and you're missing them, either your set is faulty or you're late on the set. Decreasing the distance from indicator to bugs can do the trick because you will detect strikes just a touch earlier. When guiding, I tell folks two things: if I have to say "set!" it's already too late, and sets are free, so use all you want.

The position set that I teach is a simple set that you can use any time, and as you employ it in the drift swing, you reinforce how to set nymphs naturally. It's not how hard you set, but how quickly. A quick, fluid motion that straightens the line is all it takes. I ascribe to the theory that you won't even know about 30 percent of the fish that eat (maybe higher); of the remaining 70 percent that you detect, you'll miss half; and of the half you do hook, you'll land about 75 percent. We are leaving a bunch on the table!

Refrain from setting over your head out of the water. That's a recipe for disaster. Instead, set against the fish, or from its head to its tail, usually downstream, and try to keep your bugs in the water. If you miss a fish, you can simply mend some slack to the drift, or continue the set right into a roll or full cast. The idea is to dial in, stay over the indicator, fish the indicator and the vicinity (watching for fish movement), and set!

Have Fun with It

There are other tricks you can throw into your drift. One little trick I use is to lift the bugs through the column in front of rocks, logs, or any spot a fish may be holding in front of an obstruction. You can position yourself so the obstruction is below you in the swing stage of the drift, and as your flies drift in front of the obstruction, simply lift them slowly through the water columns. This often brings a fish to eat because it simulates insect emergence or kicks in the fish's greed reflex. The greed reflex is the fish's natural predatory response to chase food that is getting away.

When fishing caddis pupae or certain emergers or soft hackles, it's not unusual for me to stop my fly rod shortly after the middle stage, at about a 30-degree angle, and swing the bugs much like you would a streamer through the remainder of the drift. When fishing caddis this way, let them sit below you at the end of the drift for a few seconds, and slowly lift your rod tip to the one-to-one position before your next cast. Both of these methods will catch fish.

I allude to fishing angles often, and we will continue to dig deeper into this throughout this book, but you can fish a run differently, without moving your feet and spooking fish, simply by changing the angles of your casts. Say, for example, I want to fish a seam in front of me a little deeper. Instead of immediately adding weight, I can take half a step upstream and cast at the same angle as before. This will typically get my flies down a little faster, and I don't have to make any adjustments other than a small step.

Maybe I want to hit the outside edge of a seam that I have been working down the middle. Instead of stepping in, I can change my casting angle from ten o'clock to eleven o'clock and quickly add a slack mend. This will allow me to hit a different portion of the same run without doing anything but changing the angle of approach. Presenting the fly at a slightly different angle can make a huge difference. By learning how to fish your base nymph rig in a myriad of situations, you begin to learn how to manipulate the drift by making subtle and not so subtle angle and distance calculations. Will I ever have to adjust weight and depth again? Yes, but not very often!

Let's imagine you see a fish just off the far bank under a canopy of low-lying branches. There's no way to shoot your bugs under the branches without snagging. Try casting a bit higher upstream than usual, as close to the brush as comfortable, and throw a downstream mend toward the bank. This mend will begin to pull your flies toward the far bank under the branches. Somewhere within the drift, well before it gets to your target fish, either pick up the slack or install an upstream mend. Maybe you're thinking that's an awful lot of movement, but remember in this case you may only need a 2-foot drift to pick up a fish. With a little practice and experimentation, this technique is a piece of cake and again illustrates that you don't always have to adjust the nymph rig if you know how to work angles.

Before you move through a seam you've been fishing to no avail, try changing your angle or adding a special technique to your presentation.

You may be surprised at the outcome. Use your imagination and have some fun with different techniques.

Xs and Os

- Keep the fly rod flat and moving at the same speed as the indicator.
- Manage your slack with the management loop.
- Mend far to near first, and micromend to hinges second.
- Keep the fly rod moving as you throw in a mend.
- Stay ahead of the drift and anticipate mends, so you don't have to play catch up.
- Know how to keep your fly rod flat to the water during the drift.
- Understand the components of a good drift.
- Develop your mind's eye and anticipate when fish will eat your bug in the drift.
- Learn to properly set the hook.
- Mend like you mean it.
- Learn to mend horizontally and vertically.

8

Game-Plan Strategies

Ever have one of those days that you just want to throw your fly box in the river and tell the fish, "Here fish, you pick which one you want!"? I think we all have. You may have to dig down into the playbook to solve what's going on subsurface. Maybe you're missing something, a clue you failed to recognize. This is a great time to employ what you know about reading the fish and the water. Learning to read the water and the fish just might give you a few clues as to what's going on and how to formulate a game plan to attack it.

You've Found 'Em, Now Catch 'Em

Armed with knowledge of a typical run and the basic needs of trout, you can go catch a few. I use my playbook to employ a systematic approach to ascertain what the fish are eating, how they're eating, and where they are eating. If you've done your homework, you realize fish are holding in a small fraction of the water a river offers. The old adage that 90 percent of the fish live in 10 percent of the water is true, so if you locate that 10 percent and don't waste time fishing the other 90 percent, you'll be well ahead of the game. This is where fly-fishing a tailwater, or freestone in certain conditions, can be tricky. With bumps and drops in flows, runs do change, so keeping a journal of where fish move in seasonal flows and water usage flows is extremely beneficial.

Where the fish are eating from day to day can and will change, so having the ability to reread the run is critical. This is where the old saying "Ya shoulda been here yesterday" comes into play. Look at how the run melts together with different flows, and use your ability to observe the nuances to find where the fish are holding. Usually they haven't gone far, unless flows change drastically.

Higher, Off-Color Water

I remember booking a full-day guide trip with one client. The night before the guide trip we had a substantial rain in the South Platte basin. Unfortunately, one of our biggest feeder creeks began to spew chocolate-milk-colored water into the main stem. Couple this phenomenon with the fact that the morning before we headed out, the powers that be bumped up the river flows by 50 cubic feet a second (cfs), and, well, let's just say things could've gone good or bad.

I made a few adjustments to the nymph rig I had been using in the days prior, in favor of a rig that was more chocolate friendly. We stepped in the river and couldn't see more than 6 inches into the water. Confident depth and speed were set correctly, we began to methodically work the edge of the flat in front of us. Both of us were surprised when we hooked and landed half a dozen fish in twice as many casts.

Not only did we catch numbers of fish that day, but we caught more than a handful of large fish. Once again, I believe that during conditions such as these, the larger fish feel more comfortable with the added camouflage, and they tend to eat more frequently and longer. Water under these conditions requires more patience and a dedicated approach to systematically covering every inch of it, but it can be worth it.

In runoff, or high-water conditions, fish can be forced to the edges of the river. In these conditions, even when the water is off color, you can pick up fish by adding weight and dredging the edges. Lots of folks get scared off by high water, but it is fishable as long as it's not

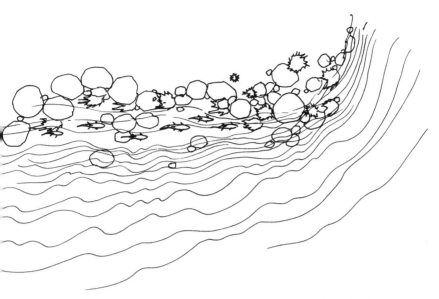

Systematically work high water from downstream to upstream along the edges.

complete chocolate and full of debris. In conditions such as these I tell folks, "The bad news is we will only be able to fish the edges; the good news is that's where the fish are." Fish larger, flashy flies such as fluorescent pink or red San Juan Worms and large, dark stonefly nymph patterns like Pat's Rubber Legs or Prince Nymphs, and don't be too timid to throw other large bugs in dark, contrasting colors. I will even dead-drift streamer patterns under the indicator followed by a large, flashy point fly.

Fish in these conditions don't have a lot of time to inspect your flies, nor do they move much laterally to chase down food, but they still have to eat. It's your job to get proper depth and speed to put the fly right on their grill. You can usually get right on top of them because of poor water clarity, so stay with short-line nymphing and ultrashort drifts. Now's a good time to employ upstream nymphing techniques to cover the upstream edges (refer to chapter 7) and a systematic approach to covering the remainder of the water. Remember to load up on the weight and be careful wading.

Looking at the illustration of high water on the previous page, you can see that on the inside bend (river right looking downstream) is a softer section that will hold fish forced to the edge under the vegetation. Set up on the lower, downstream edge at the end of the bank vegetation, and work upstream nymphing techniques to pick off fish. Work that entire edge systematically all the way up and around the inside bend.

Low-Water Conditions

The goal of this chapter is to get fly fishers to the point where they can fly-fish multiple scenarios and conditions. Low-water conditions carry as many roadblocks as high-water conditions, but everything just happens at a slower pace. Usually with low-water conditions you also have clear water to contend with. The fish are already spooky because of diminished cover, so the slightest fly rod flash or errant bug slap will send them packing.

You'd think that to combat spooky fish and low or skinny water, you would fish longer leaders, move or remove indicators, and go to lighter tippets. I'll make some changes, but they are fairly subtle. Running a three-bug nymph rig setup the way I do already places the last or point fly at about $9^1/2$ feet from the junction of the leader and fly line. I still run 5X tippets, but I ensure they are fluorocarbon. I place the indicator a minimum of about $4^1/2$ feet from the weight. To determine the weight I need, I factor in water depth, water speed, and where fish are holding to help decide how much weight I need. Sometimes, adding a weighted fly to the rig as your first dropper is all that you need.

Fly-Fishing Bathtubs

More often than not, fishing in low-water conditions forces the angler to fish pockets formed by structure. Even riffle areas have bathtubs that hold feeding fish. These areas are often visible from higher vantage points and are often as small as a bathtub. It's a good idea to survey areas from above before you move in to fish them. I enjoy getting to vantage points and directing the angler as to where to set up and place casts to pick off fish.

The trick is to find the perimeter or sides of the bathtub quickly and accurately so you don't spook the fish. You need to find the upstream side of the bathtub first. Using a tuck cast (see page 139), attempt to place your flies so they drift over the upstream side without snagging the edge. If your rig catches on the upstream side on your first cast, simply free the rig and place your next cast *directly* on the spot where you were previously snagged. After you locate the upstream perimeter, you then need to locate the farthest bathtub side. Same rule applies, if you snag it: place the next cast right on it.

Follow the same rules to find the inside perimeter, but the downstream perimeter requires a different technique. As your flies near the lower perimeter, simply lift the rig through the water columns to mimic fly emergence and to keep from snagging the lower perimeter. You can hook many fish using the lift technique at the end of a bathtub. You can pick apart on entire run of low water using this method. Find the bathtub perimeters, use short accurate presentations, and lift at the end of the drift. Repeat.

Where you set up to attack skinny water is important. Sneaking into a run while keeping a low profile and using available cover or shadows is imperative. Getting that first cast where you want it while not being discovered is key and, quite frankly, takes a lump of experience and blown opportunities. The best low-water nymph fishers are able to use angles that place only the flies in the seams, while the indicators are nearly invisible to the fish. I leave the indicator in place because if I'm going to go to all the trouble to set up, I don't want to miss a take. Low water is a fun challenge.

Highly Pressured Water

Most folks, when they think of highly pressured water, think of tailwaters. Although tailwaters receive pressure year-round, I've fished freestones that are highly pressured as well. Pressure, in my opinion, is anything that forces fish to move from typical holding lies, while changing their feeding patterns and habits.

On the South Platte we get angling, outfitting, and recreational pressure. This "bikini hatch" comes off every summer day around 10 a.m., and flotillas of tubers glide down the river. There are several free-stones that get the same pressures, and the key to success is how you change your tactics to combat the increased pressure.

Not long ago I was fishing with a couple of clients for a full-day trip. We had good success in the morning, but knew we were in for tougher times as the day wore on. After lunch, we cruised to a stretch where I know some nice fish hold. Trouble is, I'm not the only one that knows where this run is and where the fish typically hold.

We set up in the usual seams and worked them blindly for a short time. Not moving any fish, and sure we were rigged properly, we decided to move upstream to the next holding water. As we walked upstream I happened to glance to my right, and in about 6 inches of water, under an overhanging bush I spotted a large dorsal fin protruding the water. I have walked this stretch hundreds of times without ever seeing fish in there.

We adjusted the rig, positioned ourselves, and picked the fish off in about three casts. A beautiful brown trout came to net, as did another three along that bank in skinny conditions. The point is, when fish get pressured, they don't always sulk in the deepest runs; on the contrary, that's when I start looking in the next prime spots.

Look in skinny water, side seams, and faster riffles where you wouldn't expect to normally find them. Cover those areas well, and sight-fish where you can. You'd be surprised where you'll find fish in heavily pressured waters.

To further combat heavy pressure, I'll also employ a few other tested tactics. One such tactic is to fish less flashy flies. Instead of throwing a flashback RSII, I will switch to the same pattern and size, only it won't have any flash. I will also decrease tippet diameter, say from 5X to 6X to keep anything that may spook fish to a minimum. Remember to move slowly in the river, don't profile yourself on the banks, and use shadows and any other cover to blend in.

What Are They Eating?

Before we can go any further, we need to talk about discerning how fish are feeding and what they are feeding on from a nymphing perspective. Unlike watching riseforms to see how fish are feeding, discerning how fish are feeding on nymphs is a bit more complicated.

As we fly-fish with nymphs, we are concerned with what's going on with the bugs subsurface, but we also have to be aware of what adults are hatching at the same time. What bugs are hatching can give us clues about not only what nymphs the fish may be eating, but what emerger and pupa patterns we can fish as well. I like to match my nymphs, emergers, and pupa to the adults I can see. Also be aware that fish may be eating seasonal bugs, such as stonefly nymphs or egg patterns. It's always a good idea to stop at your local fly shop to get firsthand knowledge of what the fish are eating, and pick up a few bugs while you're at it.

Most times there will be some sort of hatch coming off, but what if there isn't a visible hatch? I like to flip rocks to look for clues. Other folks like to seine or pump fish to see what they're eating. Pumping fish is fine, but I suggest you refrain from it if you don't have any experience until you see how it's done, so you don't harm the fish. When I seine or flip rocks, I'm looking for nymphs that are under rocks above a run. This can go a long way in determining what type and size nymph you can pull from your fly box. Try to match size and profile first, and if you can, match the color as well.

After you get a pretty good idea of what the fish are eating, it's time to focus in on how they are eating. I break the water into three vertical columns: the lower column in the lower third, the middle column or the middle third, and the upper column including the film. The film is the top 2 inches of water that includes the surface. Ever drop a sewing needle flat on the water in a glass? It floats because the surface tension of the water can support it. Emerging insects can have a hard time breaking through that tension, which can cause them to become trapped. Because it's technically still subsurface, I consider it part of the nymphing spectrum.

Fish that are eating nymphs and larvae are typically moving laterally or swinging in the lower column. Keep an eye out for fish that are flashing as they move laterally or vertically in the water columns to feed. You may see fish exhibiting the same behaviors in the middle column, and they may be eating both nymphs and emergers or pupae. Fish that are porpoising in the upper column are probably eating emergers. A porpoising fish exposes only its dorsal fin out of the water, and you rarely see its mouth break the surface. Sometimes you'll observe a fish in the middle column or lower upper column rising to eat in the film. That's evidence it is eating something that is moving up in the column, so attack this fish with an emerger pattern or pupa to match the bugs that are hatching. If you happen to see its mouth break the surface, then the fish is most likely eating duns and we won't use a nymph rig to catch that fish on the surface. So, in short, you can tell a lot about how a fish is feeding by what column it is in and how it is feeding. The key is to identify hatching adult flies, discern how and where the fish are feeding, and then reverse engineer which stage of which bug would catch fish.

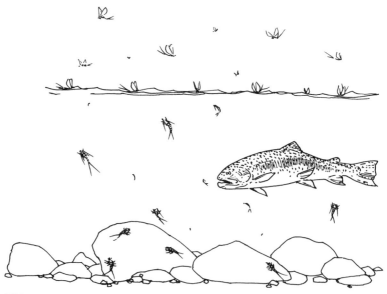

This trout is content to eat Baetis *emergers in the mid to upper columns. Rig up accordingly.*

The Systematic Approach

Let's look at nymphing a typical run. You are the offensive coordinator; it's important to have a plan in mind and stick to it. This plan needs to be consistent, duplicable, and designed around your strengths. Make sure you are rigged properly for depth, speed, profile, and color, and that you are comfortable with making quick, decisive adjustments. For purposes of this discussion, we are not concerned with what flies you are throwing as much as your systematic approach. Let's assume a mayfly hatch is beginning, specifically a Blue-Winged Olive hatch, and you are rigged with a Pheasant Tail dropper with an RSII as a point fly, all roughly the size of the adults you observe. That's a good systematic approach to reverse engineering the run you are about to nymph.

Grid System

When you step up to the run, you are already in stealth mode. You are aware of the sun's angle and your profile. Try not to cast any shadows on the river as you begin to survey the defense. Ease your way along the edge down to the tailout of the run. At this point, imagine overlaying a grid on the water surface (see the illustrations on pages 88–91). This is critical, as it will help us fish our way in, and allow you the opportunity to fish the entire run piece by piece. In most cases I will fish a run from downstream to upstream. This helps me stay behind the fish, so hopefully I'm not as easily detected. I have found over the years that the upper third of the run holds the most feeding fish, but I try to fight the urge to fish that part until I get there. Fish in and up, resisting the urge to skip water, unless you are certain you are not over fish. I've thought that I wasn't over fish many times, only to take a step and blow out a bruiser.

Fish have nature's camouflage; they are designed to be hidden from danger above, so not being able to pick out every fish is common. That is why I am so adamant about fishing your way in and up a run. With no more than 12 feet of fly line out, pick your first target point on the grid. This should be a spot upstream of you at about a 45-degree angle. Notice that I let the line out first.

I advise folks to lay out the fly line you plan to cast below you on the water before you make your initial cast. In this way, you're not flashing your fly rod in the open as you unhook your rig to cast. Set up beforehand, so all you have to do is pick up your fly rod tip, pick a spot, and roll cast your indicator on the water. Less is certainly more in this case.

After your initial drift, place a position set at the end, and calmly pick up your fly rod tip to prepare for the next roll cast. Usually I will place three or so casts through the first series of grids I can comfortably reach, take a stealthy ninja step in, and hit my next target points. In most cases, you do not need to let out more fly line. This is where folks begin to lose the game plan. Too much line forces you to expose more fish to your presence and lessens your ability to get a good drift. If you hook a fish on one of your drifts, try to move the fish downstream to land it where you've already fished in an attempt to not spook the entire pod. This can be tricky, and if you do spook other fish, wait a bit, and fish will typically move back into their holds. Continue to fish your

When you're done with the initial grid, back straight out, move upstream fifteen feet, and repeat the grid to match water characteristics.

way in, picking apart each seam, pocket, shelf, bar, eddy, and any other place fish hold. After hitting all of the points in this set, back straight out quietly, move upstream 15 feet, and repeat the process.

Tempo, tempo, tempo. There is a rhythm to nymphing. As you work the grid, try to get in a rhythm where you are smoothly covering the water with each drift, and each preceding drift sets up the next one. The more fluid you are, the more relaxed you are, and the more fish you'll pick up. Trust me.

If you know you're fishing over fish, but they are not eating, check your depth and speed to ensure you are in the proper vertical columns. If you are satisfied with depth and speed and are fairly sure you have the correct bugs, try switching your flies' color or profile, or switch to a smaller version of what your are throwing. Try to change flies once for every five depth and speed changes.

Alternate Grid Patterns

Thankfully, not all of the runs in a river are typical, so you have to modify your grid to match what the river is giving you. If I am fishing a run that has tightly compressed seams, pools or glass, and other characteristics, I will adjust the grid to match. In faster moving water, the grid lines are closer together, as close as 6 inches, to ensure proper coverage. I want to fish that water effectively. For pool and pockets where the water is moving slower, and depending on bottom structure (more structure means a tighter grid), I will set up a grid from 12 to 24 inches apart. It all depends on how well you can read the water and what the run presents.

I approach pocketwater the same way, as it usually presents a seam with faster moving water, a slower moving pocket, and another faster moving seam. You should fish your way in using tight grids in the faster water, and farther spaced grids for the pocket.

When you fish the pocket section, place your flies a foot or so downstream of the obstruction causing the pocket. Too many times I see anglers trying to cast above it and drift it that way. Add some

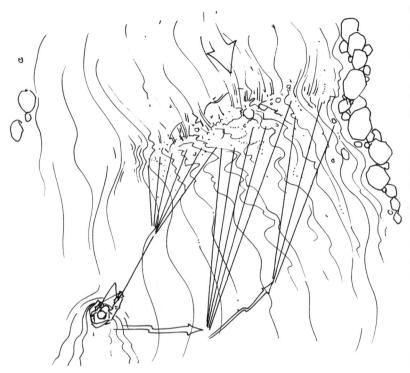

Work your way up and in. Notice in the illustration how you can cast below the obstruction, and simply change cast angles to cover the water.

weight, hit a couple feet downstream of it, and high-stick it through the pocket, keeping fly line off of the near seam.

When fishing multiple pockets in a run, it's best to approach from downstream with a plan. You don't want to paint yourself in a corner here, so study the run a bit to formulate the best approach path. Depending on the configuration of the pockets, pick a side that offers the best approach and hit the nearest seam of the nearest pocket. After fishing that seam, hit the adjoining pocket and then the connected seam. Next, move to a position that allows you to fish the next seam, pocket, and seam of the closest pocket to your position. Continue up the run fishing each seam and pocket you encounter. Be sure to look for seams between pockets, as they can carry a lot of food and hold several

Big Nasty San Juan Worm (recipe on page 153)

Beadhead Soft-Hackle Pheasant Tail (recipe on page 153)

Brachy Pupa (Caddis) (recipe on page 153)

Girl Scout (recipe on page 153)

Periwinkle (recipe on page 153)

Brown RSII (Chocolate Thunder) (recipe on page 153)

Split Case PMD (recipe on page 154)

Black Beauty (recipe on page 154)

Mamba Midge Pupa (recipe on page 154)

South Platte Shimmer Midge (recipe on page 154)

Graphic Caddis (recipe on page 154)

Mercer's Beadhead Golden Biot Stonefly (recipe on page 154)

fish. It's sad but true—I often hum "You've Got to Pick a Pocket or Two" from *Oliver*.

Bends are great for fishing with the grid approach. Like I mentioned earlier, bends tend to force two or more seams into one slot. Also, bends are great places for shelves, bars, and eddies to form, thus giving the fish great holds to pick off insects. The key to gridding a bend is to align the grid with the angle that is formed as the water transitions from a straight path to the bend. I fish my way into a bend from downstream to upstream, usually at an angle that matches the gridlines.

The key to fishing this or any other shelf is to have enough weight and depth to come off the shelf at fish level and still put the flies on the shelf without constantly hanging on the bottom. Usually 3 feet or so is all the farther you have to cast onto the shelf to get your bugs where you

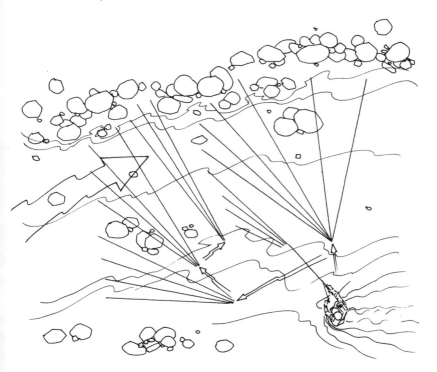

Bend grid placement and attack angles. Fish from near to far and "ninja" your way in.

want them, provided your weight is correct. This will get your bugs to tumble down the shelf. Of course, there are other variables at work here, so some experimentation may be in order. After you do this enough, it becomes old hat. Remember, the faster the water, the tighter the grid.

Sight-Nymphing

The grid pattern is great for blind-nymphing, or fishing in water where you can't see the fish. I also employ the grid system when I see fish activity out in front of me and I still want to fish my way in. This is a bit different from sight-nymphing, because in sight-nymphing I can see my target. Depending on how far away my target fish is and how big it is, I may still fish my way in. If I locate a large fish for a client, we ease our way in, looking for sentry fish. Sentry fish are usually subordinate fish that stand between you and a target fish. Try not to spook those fish because they can bolt and flush your target. If you're looking for a challenge, try to roll a few sentry fish on the way in to the target fish!

Fish see about as well as we do underwater. They have binocular vision, a large peripheral zone, and can see above in a cone configuration, or cone zone. Fish have peripheral view of about 300 degrees, more than twice that of humans. How well they can spot you depends on other factors, such as sun angle, cloud cover, and water surface turbulence or chop.

I have read so many articles over the years that explain how fish see that even my vision was blurred. The way I look at it is this: if a fish can see my feet in the water, it can probably see my head and can certainly see the flash of my fly rod and fly line. To minimize my outline, I move slowly, try to put the chop between me and the fish, and prepare the line for a roll cast before I approach my target. Regardless of whether I have a target fish on the radar, you will see me holding the rod with the proper amount of line out, horizontal and downstream, as I stalk a fish or a run.

There are times that I know a fish sees me, and it just doesn't care. Those fish can be tough to catch. In this circumstance I tell my client,

"He's on to us," and we move on. Other times, I bump a fish, follow it to its new hold, give it a few minutes, move into position, and catch that fish on the first drift. With experience, you will begin to learn the nuances of getting close to fish. From experience, with my height of 5 feet 10 inches, I feel I can get to within about 15 feet of a fish in 2 feet of water, depending on conditions. Someday, when fishing is slow, or you want to have some fun, experiment to see how close you can get to fish at various depths, water conditions, and sky conditions.

Sometimes I guide accomplished fly fishers. On these days, I spend most my time spotting and netting fish. These folks have figured out how to set up and drift to a target fish. They instinctively know how close they can get, while they set up slightly downstream from the fish. As a rule you want to get as close as you can to minimize drag, add enough weight that you can put your flies about 3 feet above the fish and hit their position in the vertical column, and keep casting to a minimum. You may only get one shot.

When casting to a target fish, only one grid line leads right to the fish's face. It is important that it sees only the flies and tippet. Once it sees your indicator or fly line, it can mean game over. The better you get at sight-nymphing, the more line you can keep between your indicator and dropper fly. As a general rule, when you are learning this skill, keep about 4 feet of line between your indicator and your dropper or first fly. Use the $1^{1}/_{2}$ times indicator to fly length to set your depth for any water more than 2 feet deep. When you cast, notice where your flies hit in relation to the fish, and if your drift will take you outside of your target, you can simply pull your flies toward you to line them up with the fish. Many times, after we spot a fish, I will take my guest up- or downstream to practice this skill. We simply pick out a rock in similar water and work for a brief time before going back to take a crack at the fish.

Alright, so we see a fish, we sneak in with the amount of line we need trailing below us, cast 3 feet above the fish, and quickly take up slack and get our fly rod low and flat above the water. Now here is where I differ from some folks regarding the sight-nymph drift. I will point my fly rod tip about a foot below or downstream of my indicator.

I do this for two reasons: One is so I have an unobstructed view of the entire scene. The other reason is that I can set much quicker.

Remember, your drift will be only about 4 to 8 feet, so if you take up slack quickly, drag is not an issue. Also, when I sight-fish, I am looking mainly at the fish, and the indicator is in my peripheral vision. If that fish moves side to side, up or down, or opens its mouth, I am in perfect position to set. Fish eat and spit faster than a baby, so I want to have an unobstructed, ringside seat to observe it. Sight-fishing is a blast; it's the ultimate nymphing experience, and it requires both basic and advanced skills to master.

Mastering the 3-Foot Drift

In my opinion, sight-fishing is a close game. The closer I can get to my target, the less line I need, and the less movement required for the perfect presentation. It's the epitome of nymphing because I have to apply pretty much everything I know to be successful. I have to be able to sight the fish, sneak into position, present the correct flies in the correct column at correct speeds, and set on movement. I call it mastering the 3-foot drift.

Again, familiarity with your nymph rig breeds consistency. I have to know exactly where the flies will be within the drift at every point to become a successful sight-nympher. You must be able to master short drifts.

What's so tough about short drifts? Short drifts mean close fish and much less room for error. You have to be able to calculate how far upstream you must cast above a sighted fish to get the flies right on that fish's grill. To do this, you must read the fish's depth and the speed of the water and be able to discern any flow characteristics that may change the drift. In other words, even though you may have the speed and depth figured out, you still need to read the water again to make sure you don't need to take additional steps to get a perfect drift.

Spend some time next time you're on the river just watching fish feed. You will notice a lot, but I think the most important characteristic you'll notice is the way fish move side to side to eat. This is important to know because as mentioned before, the actual act of a fish eating your flies is not always telegraphed to the indicator, especially while sight-nymphing, so your ability to recognize an eat is paramount.

Depending on where and how you have to set up on a particular fish, you may not see the actual eat, so you need to set on movement—not just any movement, but appropriate movement. Freddy Adamany (a longtime client) and I were set up perfectly on a fish one day. In this instance, the flies needed to be placed in the right seam only about 4 feet upstream of the fish to get the right depth and speed. Freddy presented perfectly.

Much of the time, when setting up on a large fish with the client amped up with excitement, I rarely say anything as the fish eats in hopes to prevent the client from setting too hard and subsequently snapping off. I watched that fish move a foot to the right, eat and spit the flies, swing back to its original hold, and Freddy never set. "Why in the world did you not set?" I asked. Freddy yelled back at me, "Because I was too busy watching him eat!"

When you watch fish eat nymphs, generally they will move out of their hold, swing to the insect, eat, and immediately swing back to their hold. You set as they begin to swing back to their original hold. If they move up in the column to eat, set as they begin to move back down to where they started. These are just guidelines, but setting on those movements beats just watching them eat . . . like Freddy.

I love the 3-foot drift because it's about stealth and calculations more than it is about mending. Once you master picking off fish with nymphs at close ranges, you will begin to fill the net each time out.

Accomplished Nymph Fishers

People often ask me how I would define an advanced or accomplished nympher. I've been lucky enough to fly-fish with some of the best around, and there is a vast difference between advanced and other levels of nymph fishers.

First off, those with advanced skills approach the river with a consistent rig. I've said it many times, but I can't stress enough how important it is to fish one nymph rig for a long duration. You begin to see where the bugs are throughout the drift and make adjustments based on dynamic options, not guesses. Advanced nymphers attack the river with a systematic, consistent approach of reading water, fish, and flies, while picking it apart with tempo. One drift sets up the next, and the advanced fisher makes subtle changes in casting angles to place the bugs at various levels of coverage before moving to the next nuance of the same seam.

They aren't necessarily the best fly casters, but they can roll a 20-foot cast right where they are looking. They are good at mending, but most of the time they fish a high, flat stick with a touch of slack line. Finally, they are attentive to detail but not hamstrung by it. They realize it's all about the bugs in the proper seam at the proper speed and depth.

These characteristics can apply to intermediate nymph fishers. There is a distinction that truly sets advanced from intermediate fly fishers. It's all about presentation and set. It's all about ensuring that your flies are precisely on the fish's face, and setting on everything. I have guided clients who can present flies excellently, but what they lack is the set. I've described my preferred method to physically set, but it's more than that. It comes down to what to set on.

Beginners often tell me that they didn't feel a thing after they missed a set. I'm talking about when I tell them to set, they don't, and then they say they felt nothing. Those folks are still learning and are quite easy to help once you get the point across that they won't feel the fish until after the set. But those who don't set in obvious conditions are difficult to fix and at times frustrating.

Often I tell someone to set only to have them explain, "That wasn't a fish, only the bottom." These are usually the intermediate folks who have caught fish in the past in conditions that made hookups easier. Most times, as advanced folks know, you have to be all over the indicator and set on everything. Jeremy Hyatt asks folks why they are arguing with the indicator. It's telling them when to set.

The best nymph fishers I've fished with rarely make it through an entire drift without a set somewhere. Every drift, all day. Amazing how many fish they pick up. They set every time the indicator doesn't float naturally, whether it's a pause, twitch, plunge, or a slight rotation. If you want to get everything out of your day on the water, do what the best do: concentrate on the presentation and set. Present and set.

Skinny Rig

The skinny rig is typically used for catching fish that are eating emergers subsurface. I refer to it as skinny not because of low-water conditions, but because of the upper water column you fish it in. You're "skinny" under the surface. For a large portion of the prime fly-fishing season, whether I'm guiding or fishing on my own, I carry a spare rod rigged with a dry or dry-dropper setup. This is for the times of the season where nymphing is effective all day, but it's a good bet that sometime during the day the fish will begin to eat adult and emergent stages of certain insects. Because the South Platte is a finicky tailwater, hatches don't always happen at once or last long. Snipping a three-bug nymph rig and switching to a dry-dropper that we might fish for only ten to fifteen minutes just doesn't make a ton of sense. I carry a prerigged spare for this special time.

A couple years ago, I neglected to grab my spare rod from the truck before our trip, and lo and behold, we found ourselves in the middle of an epic Blue-Winged Olive (BWO) hatch. (We sometimes call them "Blue Wings" in the circles I fish.) Fish were either gently sipping the duns or they were rolling on the emergers slightly subsurface. We were too far from the vehicle to go get another rig and not feeling confident that this hatch and feeding frenzy would continue, so I tried something different.

That particular day, I was nymphing a three-bug rig under a yarn indicator—my typical rig. The top fly was a red San Juan Worm, followed by a Soft-Hackled Pheasant Tail, topped off with a brown BWO emerger pattern. I removed all of the nymphing weight, slid the indicator to about 5 feet from the top fly, and used floatant to grease the red San Juan Worm. The adjustments took only seconds, and we worked over several nice fish.

The skinny rig was born, but I wasn't confident that it was a function of the rig or the amazing fish-feeding frenzy that caused its success. Since that day, I have used the skinny rig a hundred times. It works, but you have to follow some important keys for it to succeed.

First off, you have to match the phase of the bug the fish are eating. Whether it's a BWO emerger or a Caddis pupa, you have to have a likely representation of the bug in your rig. Second, you need the skill to accurately present the bug in the right column at the right speed with zero drag. Third, you have to be able to set up as close to the fish as possible without them spooking. Last, you have to be able to provide a full, gentle set. Sounds easy enough, I'm sure, but let me expand.

I like to have a large, lightweight attractor bug in my skinny rig. Most days a red San Juan will fit the bill as my initial dropper because my clients and I can locate and track the bug throughout the drift. This bug also takes on floatant well and will stay close to the surface for long durations provided your drift is relatively drag-free. There are dozens of BWO emerger patterns out there, but I like an RSII in brown, gray, or black as my point fly. My middle bug is typically a Soft-Hackled Pheasant Tail or Hare's Ear. The soft hackles are especially deadly on the swing portion of this rig because they are close to the surface and mimic emerging flies or pupa. Just cover all of the food groups.

I put some forethought into how I'll set up my nymph rig for the day with an eye toward using the skinny rig. I still tie everything on 5X fluoro tippet, use eye-to-eye connections where appropriate, and use weight that I can adjust or remove quickly. I fish it consistently throughout the year. Because this is my go-to rig, I have a pretty good idea, after all of these years, where my flies will be at all times in the drift.

The ability to predict where your flies will be in the column based on rig setup and water speed is critical. This comes from experience and using the same rig over and over.

I grease the San Juan Worm for two reasons: one is to help keep the other two bugs close to the surface, and the other is to help my clients see the bugs during the drift. Once you locate a target fish, you have to decide how far upstream you will cast to ensure the proper fly is at the proper depth, drag-free, when it gets to the fish. Estimate how fast the water is flowing and how far upstream of the fish you will have to place the bugs to get the right depth as you get to the fish. Keep drifts short.

I have used the skinny rig with numerous people over the years, and most have a tendency to over-cast and over-drift. Most, if not all drifts, are under 5 feet long. Several are only 2 feet in length. If the fish is feeding on or just below the surface, I have to put the flies at eye level or above eye level to the fish to elicit an eat. This means that casts are short and accurate, and drifts are short and quick.

Most of the time, I set up slightly downstream of the intended fish and as close as I can get. If the river is flowing left to right, I'll try to set my clients with their left shoulder even with the fish's tail as it faces upstream. Most skinny rig casts are less than 20 feet, depending on the water surface chop disrupting the fish's view. Pick one fish. That's key. If given a few chances, you can dial in the rig depth and speed quickly by using one fish as a gauge. If only one fish is feeding, you can go right at it, or you can fish your way into it by taking a few practice drifts on your way in. You can also time the fish if it's in a fairly stable feeding pattern and place a cast upstream at the proper distance to match the fish's feeding interval.

I like the slightly downstream setup for several reasons: most importantly it puts me in perfect position for a quick, gentle set because the drift is so short. I'm sure you can use upstream and quartering stream approaches, but on this water under these circumstances, this works best for me. Pick a spot above or upstream of the fish, gauge the speed of the water, and cast so only the flies are seen by the fish. Maybe you're wondering by now why I leave the indicator on. Folks, me included, simply miss some takes, and the indicator will help show you a few you otherwise would miss as it stops abruptly.

You've placed a perfect cast the perfect distance upstream of your quarry. Now what? Watch the fish. You have a visible bug floating to the fish—watch that and the fish's movement. One mechanical tactic that works here is putting the rod tip about a foot downstream of the indicator just like you would anytime you're sight-fishing. It shortens the distance of the set and gives you full view of the fish's reactions. You're looking for the fish to move side to side or up to eat your flies. The drift is so short that more often than not you see everything straighten out as the fish eats your offering. Otherwise, set on the fish as it swings to the bugs or you see its mouth open. Set gently, because the fish will most often take off once it realizes it's been tricked, and you don't have any weight on the rig to absorb the force of the set. A lot of folks snap off at this point, so prepare yourself for a smooth, soft, downstream, low-angled lift.

The skinny rig lends itself to fishing to one particular fish or blind-nymphing to several feeding fish. It's useful as you begin to figure out how far to cast upstream of feeding fish. Again, consistency with one nymph rig setup is crucial as you begin to know exactly where your bugs will be in the columns at various points in the drift. Couple this with the ability to sneak in with the proper flies for the conditions, the skills to attain a short, drag-free drift, and the ability to set smoothly, and then having to carry two rods to match all the conditions may be a thing of the past.

The ability to properly fish the river is key. The simple fact that you are approaching the river with a workable, versatile, and systematic approach can be the difference in how many fish you catch. This approach will help you evolve from a beginner and will enhance your skills as an accomplished fly fisher. If you follow this game plan, not only will it open more doors for you, but it will certainly allow you to walk away from a day nymphing the river knowing that you fished well.

Xs and Os

- Use a systematic approach to learn what, where, and how fish are eating.
- Develop the ability to effectively fly-fish various water conditions.
- Learn to break the water into three vertical columns.

- Understand how and where in the columns fish typically eat nymphs, larvae, pupae, and emergers.
- Learn to use the grid system to systematically pick apart runs on any section of river.
- Learn to fly-fish bathtubs.
- Develop the ability to sight-nymph.
- Learn to fish the skinny rig.

9

Stillwater Still Runs

When most think of fly fishing and nymphing in general, they think about moving water. I haven't seen too much written about nymphing stillwater, but I've done a bunch of it over the years. I'm talking about climbing into a small pontoon, belly boat, or float tube and catching fish subsurface by nymphing bugs under an indicator.

My son Parker learned to fly-fish from a belly boat or float tube. It was a great way for him to stay involved, have some fun floating in the water, and it helped his casting and line management skills. Since you're isolating your upper torso in a float tube, you can concentrate on the casting action. His casting quickly evolved from a simple, down-angled roll cast with a high fly rod tip, to a full backcast. Having water at your waist and water behind you helps you focus on keeping the rod tip in the proper casting plane and control the loop and tempo. You quickly develop proper casting mechanics if you continually slap and splash water in front and behind you.

As for the float tube, I still use my original purchase, a tricked out round belly boat that has seen a bunch of water time. You don't see those much anymore; you're more likely to see the V hull design. Most of my clients use that design and explain that they are easy to get in

Greg Smits enjoys time on the lake in a float tube.

and out of, place you at the proper height above the water, maneuver easily, and are extremely comfortable. Whichever design you choose, please wear a personal floatation device as well.

As for line mechanics, you learn quickly to flatten out the fly rod to the water, mend slack as needed, and lift abruptly but gently on strikes. If the angle of your fly rod is anything but horizontal over the water, not only is it counterproductive, it's just plain uncomfortable. It's much easier to rest your forearms on the front of the tube, thus keeping the fly rod flat. You quickly master adding slack to the drift because you can tell quite easily when your indicator is dragging and causing wakes. The takes can range from subtle bumps and rotations of the indicator to flat-out, line-screaming grabs that leave you speechless—and flyless, too—if you don't set properly.

Sets are simply long lifts opposite the direction the fish is going with your flies. It's not tough to figure out which direction a fish took your flies as he ate, so you learn to lift in the opposite direction. Fighting the fish on the rod is virtually the same as landing a fish on moving water; however, you will naturally keep your rod elbow up and in position unless you want it to get wet. Getting the fish to the net is something you'll just have to practice, but most folks new to fly fishing from a float tube or pontoon reel in too much line as they prepare to bag the fish. You have to catch a bunch of fish to master netting from a tube or pontoon.

My stillwater rig is comprised of a two-bug tandem under an indicator, usually tied to a 9-foot, 6-weight rod. I prefer a 6-weight fly rod with a fast action for open water because of the likelihood of encountering wind. That rod makes it easier to cut through the wind. Typically, I use a 9-foot leader tapered to 4X or 5X, add another 18 inches or so of 5X tippet below it with a double surgeon's knot, and top it off with a Styrofoam float that's about half an inch in diameter, has a small hole drilled through it, and is painted fluorescent pink. I don't often use yarn indicators when stillwater nymphing because the lakes I fish are wind-whipped most of the day. The Styrofoam ball indicator, because of its profile, is less likely to be affected by the wind than a higher profile, and lighter, yarn indicator. To affix the ball indicator to the leader, simply build a loop bunny ear, push it through the hole of the indicator, and pull the rest of the leader, tippet, and flies through the loop. Once everything is through, simply pull the leader on both sides of the ball to get the connection inside the ball. This will not only keep it from sliding down the leader, but it helps center the leader directly under the indicator and makes for quicker strike detection. Everything else looks like my normal nymph rig, with a few differences.

You still need to read the water and adjust your mechanics to allow for depth, speed, profile, and color. Don't be misled—there are certainly undercurrents that you need to deal with, and the quicker you familiarize yourself with your particular water, the better. Unlike nymphing a river, you don't need to add weight to match flow speeds. Weight in this case is designed to get your flies under the indicator quickly and keep them there. I will add weight as winds come up to help ground the indicator because I don't want my flies moving at water surface speeds. You usually don't need much weight, and most of the time a BB-size weight will do the trick.

My objective is to get my flies in the correct water columns to pick off feeding fish. This is where depth calculations are important. Since we're not drifting per se, you can usually use trial and error to get the right depth. Just keep adjusting depth until you find fish or the bottom. My bottom fly is typically set to ride just above the weed line. If you can see the bottom, this job becomes much simpler, and easier yet as you begin to pick off fish. As you begin to learn specific depths of areas where you are having success catching fish, you can then go to the next step, which is to set up to accentuate the drift.

More often than not, that bottom fly is a chironomid pattern, usually a size 16 or so. That bug matches the large midge pupa that is prevalent where I fish. The bug above the point fly can range from a damselfly nymph to a *Callibaetis* emerger. I tie this fly eye-to-eye to ensure it keeps a flat profile in the water to mimic swimming or emerging. Watching the adults hatching, figure out at what depths the fish are

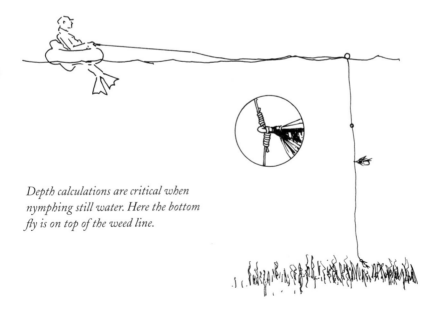

Depth calculations are critical when nymphing still water. Here the bottom fly is on top of the weed line.

feeding, and reverse engineer your final selections. Pretty basic stuff when it comes to matching fly profile and color.

I've been fishing the same lakes for years, so I have a good idea where and how I want to set up and fish. I have found that not only do I like to keep the bottom fly riding inches above the weed line, but I also like to try to fish along the weed line. I'll set up, trying to place myself where the wind will help push me and the tube through a desired path. My favorite strategy is to take some time and effort to kick into the wind above the weed edge I plan to drift, and let the wind push me right down it. When I hook fish using this method, I always make a mental note of at least two landmarks at 90 degrees and the depth of the fly the fish ate. The more fish you catch, the more dialed in you become.

I don't usually enjoy fly fishing in windy conditions, but when it comes to stillwater nymphing, I accept it. Not only does it help with the drift as I explained, but it provides chop on the water that consequently makes the indicator bob, thus moving those bugs up and down in the column. I won't say I've never nymphed a few fish in steel-calm conditions, but I can say nymphing the chop is ultimately better. The wind makes those bugs come to life. I also plan how I will fish the wind in accordance to hatch conditions. Later in the morning, after the hatch, I'll kick over to a windward side bank. This is where I'll find huge concentrations of spent, cripple, and drowned bugs. Fish, too. It's a great time to switch out a few bug patterns, adjust the weight and depth, and catch fish feeding on freebies.

On calmer days when there is less wind, I think "move the tip or strip." In other words, if Mother Nature isn't helping with providing bug life through the wind, you have to facilitate. A simple jigging motion has brought me several fish. Simply lift the fly rod tip a foot or two and let the bugs drop. Another method of inciting fish is to slightly strip a bit of line in. Generally, I'll move the indicator only a couple inches at a time when stripping in line. Almost any method of imparting motion to your flies will work; you just have to experiment.

Probably the biggest trout I ever fooled with a fly rod came from another technique that I learned from my dad over forty years ago. I typically use this method from the shore, but I have also used it out on the water. I fish a single fly on the end of a 9-foot leader. Most often, the bug I use is a scud pattern, pink or orange, and only weighted by the copper ribbing on the fly. Find a spot where the wind is blowing perpendicular to you, cast at a quartering angle into the wind, and allow the wind to drift that bug for you. Keep the fly rod low and flat over the water, watch the fly line for subtle strikes, and mend it like you would as if you're drifting a river. When the fly line gets past a 45-degree angle below you, slowly strip in and then cast again. Once you hook a fish, make a mental note of the depth where the hookup occurred and duplicate. This method has worked wonders for me for many years.

It's not unusual to wade into the lake or fish from its banks effectively—I did it all the time as a kid. It is amazing how well you can work a lake from the bank or from bars or shelves that protrude into the lake.

As in moving water, fish in lakes still need food, oxygen, and shelter. Read the water to find your fish. Unlike moving water where the insects come to the fish, for the most part in stillwater the fish are moving to the bugs. It's not unusual to see the same fish cruising a certain area several times in one day. That's its beat or territory, and it will feed in that area as conditions merit. Locate an area that has the most fish cruising their beats, set up properly, and fish it properly.

Depending on the depth of the water, you can usually locate shelves, bars, and ledges where fish like to hold. Once you locate those areas, find the vegetation lines and depth and you're well ahead of the game. Maximum depth to effectively nymph is around 10 feet. I'd say the majority of fish I catch are at 4 to 9 feet below the surface. Simple indicator depth adjustments are all you need to dial into the fish depths. Fishing obstructions will also prove fruitful. Just look for logs, rocks, or other objects that fish tend to gravitate toward.

One lake in particular has the perfect bottom topography for how I like to attack the fish. The upwind corner has a large 3- to 5-foot deep cove protected from the wind and fed by a small stream. About 60 feet from shore, a shelf forms along the cove edge. This structure allows

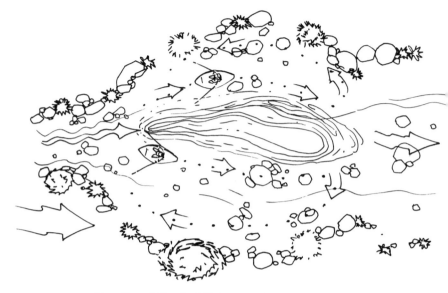

Two clients fishing in drift boats on either side of a lateral bar.

fish to feed in the cove and along the shelf that also offers protection and a weed line. Sounds good right? Well, it gets better. Perpendicular to the cove shelf is a shallow lateral bar that meanders all the way across the lake. Each side of the bar has a weed-lined shelf as well. The beauty of this situation is that one can fish the cove, the cove shelf, and finally the lateral bar, picking up fish all the while. Again, simple depth adjustments, and lining up properly to use the wind to help you drift is all you need.

On that particular lake, I typically place a client on either side of the lateral bar tucked up against the cove shelf. Here he will fish the cove shelf and then slip down each side of the lateral bar (like in the illustration above). After getting to the end of the bar on the far shore, he kicks back up to the cove and repeats the process. It works, but it took me a while to figure it out. The fun part is that you just have to keep fishing the lakes to figure them out. That's a good problem to have.

Once you float or wade a particular lake a few times, you begin to discover which areas contain the most fish. Again, it's imperative you look for protruding rocks or stumps, overhanging brush or trees, and always prevailing wind. Once you combine all of the factors and characteristics, you begin to formulate the best options for fishing each lake. It may take a few trips to figure it all out, but it can be done. Especially with a nymph rig.

Xs and Os

- Use a systematic approach to learn what, where, and how fish are eating in still water.
- Develop the ability to rig effectively for still water.
- Learn to locate areas that hold fish.
- Understand how you can use topography and wind currents to your benefit.
- If you've never fly-fished still water, give it a try!

10

Marrying Entomology

Entomology is the scientific study of insects. Many books have been written about entomology and trout fishing, and I am sure plenty more will follow. It's an immense subject. Entomology and how it relates to trout fishing needs to be a part of your playbook. I view it as an integral part of the entire playbook; how you marry it to the other basic tenets of nymphing is vital. The playbook is designed to mesh your skills, strengths, and knowledge together to work as one unit; therefore, a working knowledge of entomology is a key component to creating a comprehensive playbook while becoming a better angler.

The ability to discern *what stage of what bug* the fish are eating is the foundation of nymphing; putting that bug down the slot with a perfect presentation seals the deal. We have discussed at length how to discern where, how, and what fish are eating. Now comes the time to try and match the insect with a biological imposter.

You don't need to be a fly geek to attack a stream. You just need to know what to look for, how to match it, and how to fish it. There are four classes of bugs that nymph fishers should study: caddis, mayflies, stoneflies, and midges. Getting a solid handle on identifying these insects and their life cycles will pay huge dividends for beginners and advanced fly fishers alike.

Mayflies

Let's look at mayflies first. Ephemeroptera (mayflies) comprises 21 families and more than 600 species in North America. That's a lot of bugs! The key is to learn the common families in your area from the following *nymph* characteristics. Mayfly nymphs can be classified as swimmers, crawlers, clingers, or burrowers.

Swimmers have torpedo-shaped bodies suited for swimming, a round head, and two tails. This includes *Baetis* and *Callibaetis* (lake version).

Crawlers have a more muscular body suited for maneuvering underwater, a blockish head, and three tails. Crawling mayfly nymphs include Pale Morning Duns (PMDs), Drakes, Quills, and Tricos to name a few.

Clingers possess muscular, rectangular bodies for clinging to vegetation and also have three tails. The Western March Brown, prolific in the upper West, is an example of a clinger mayfly nymph.

Burrowing mayfly nymphs have large, stout bodies for burrowing and also sport three tails. Burrowers are predominantly an Eastern mayfly. Do you see a pattern here? That's right—count the tails, and look at the body shape. Combine that knowledge with the ability to accurately identify the adult stage of each nymph, and you've got it.

Mayflies have incomplete metamorphosis, which means they progress from egg to nymph to adult. This progression is important to the nymph fisher because we concentrate on nymph stages *and* the process from nymph to adult, or the emergence phase. During emergence, the nymph swims toward the surface to hatch into a dun or young adult. Although we are only concentrating on the first two stages as nymph fishers, it is important to know that after the bug hatches into a dun, it then molts into an adult or spinner, mates, and eventually falls dead or spent.

At this point we could keep digging and digging into mayfly entomology, but I am shooting for you to have a practical working knowledge; therefore, we will put the above information to use. In the areas I fish, *Baetis* begins coming off in March (see the hatch chart on pages

126 to 127). There are several variations in the family Baetidae, and this gives these little mayflies several different names. I've heard them called two-tailed mayflies, Blue-Winged Olives (BWOs), small quills, Baetids, and simply Blue Wings. As in any playbook, using the same terminology is important, so I choose to call them BWOs. You can distinguish them from other bugs, especially large midges, by the way they fly (usually tail down) and their sailboat-shaped wings, long and slender bodies, and two tails. Practice identifying them midair and you'll become good at it. Be mindful that with BWOs, depending on your location and time of year, the little mayfly will have different colored bodies, and their wings may not be blue at all. You may have to catch a few to get a good look. Once I discern what is coming off, I work backward to the proper nymph to match the adult. The ability to work in reverse is critical. If you can identify the adult, you can deduce the nymph. Couple that knowledge with how the fish are feeding, and you can select options without guessing. In other words, you attack the defense with your best offense.

Knowing that BWOs are swimmer nymphs with slender profiles, I select a nymph that carries that profile and size. BWOs, where I fish, are predominantly size 18 to 24. If you want to double-check their size, flip a few rocks. My favorite fly to use is a Pheasant Tail to mimic the nymph. I use other patterns, but I most often start with a Pheasant Tail. I like the Sawyer's Pheasant Tail because it has a slim profile that best matches the nymphs on the rivers I fish. I also use a gray RSII to do the job as well. The RSII is a fantastic bug with a great profile, and it can also be fished as an emerger. Whenever you throw an RSII or another emerger pattern, concentrate on the swing phase of your drift. Fish can be induced to eat as the fly rises through the columns. Other BWO nymph patterns I use include:

- Randy Smith's *Baetis*
- Periwinkle
- Skinny Nelson
- Flashback, Beadhead, and Mercury Pheasant Tails
- Olive Micro Mayfly
- Periwinkle (can be used as a midge larva as well)

- Split Case BWO
- Whitley's Sparkle Wing RSII (gray or olive, fished as a nymph or emerger)
- Olive Hare's Ear (slim profile)
- 2 Bit Hooker
- Craven's Ju Ju *Baetis* (fished as a nymph or emerger)
- Sawyer's Pheasant Tail

When I notice fish in the middle or upper columns feeding during a Blue-Winged Olive hatch, I dig into my fly box in search of patterns that match the emergence phase. Some of my favorite mayfly emerger patterns include:

- Gray or olive RSII
- Whitley's Sparkle RSII
- Barr's Emergers and Barr's Beadhead Emergers
- BWO Loopwing
- Soft-Hackle Pheasant Tails
- Solitude's Copper-Ribbed RSII (aka Chocolate Thunder)

I have become a fan of soft hackles. I use them quite often before and during a hatch. Soft hackles resemble the emergence phase of the bug and can be dead-drifted or swung. They can be a great addition to any fly box because they are versatile. Although soft hackles have been around for many years, I don't see them being used as often as other patterns, yet trout gobble them up.

What I like about fishing with mayfly patterns, *Baetis* in particular, is that they have a lot of crossover; in other words, you can run the RSII, one of my favorite patterns, as a nymph and as an emerger. *Baetis* nymphs are active, swim well, and move throughout all of the water columns before, during, and after a hatch. An RSII or Solitude's Copper-Ribbed RSII, which I affectionately call the Chocolate Thunder, is a good choice to fish in any column during a hatch. These flies mimic the profiles well, and you can place them as emerger droppers and nymphs in your rig effectively. The RSII and the Chocolate Thunder are the two best flies to use for the skinny rig (see page 97) because of the characteristics of the mayfly and the design of the flies.

Now's a good time to discuss what I call fly fatigue. I'm not sure who is affected more, the fish or the fisherman, but fly fatigue is real on heavily pressured waters. Sometimes I will find a hot bug that works day in and day out for an extended period. Suddenly, the fish begin to refuse it, or in some cases, run from it, even though conditions are perfect. The patterns I've listed above are similar in size and profile, but when fish begin to refuse, I try a smaller size of the hot bug or go to a different pattern altogether. Soft hackles and subtle changes in color, contrast, profile, and size are, in my opinion, great ways to fight fly fatigue.

As for crawling, clinging, and burrowing mayfly nymphs, most have more bulk, bigger heads, three tails, and larger profiles. Again, you can effectively fish various columns and bug stages in one rig. One exception to large bulky mayflies is the *Tricorythodes*, or Trico. This tiny mayfly is a favorite trout food during this hatch, and it will give you fits if you can't identify it. Look for tiny mayflies with a brown, black, or green body and three tails.

Fishing during a Trico hatch can be gloriously frustrating. The black male Trico usually hatches in the late evening. The gray or olive females usually hatch in the morning as the males are forming large swarming columns above the water. The females meet the males, mate, and then fall spent. What could be so frustrating about that? Well, as they fall spent, the sheer number of them will not only blow your mind, but the fishes' as well. In other words, the fish become totally dialed in to eating just the spents. How in the world does a nymph fisher get in on this action?

First off, a lot goes on prior to the flies falling spent. When I know the Tricos are coming off, I nymph with a black RSII in the evenings to match the male hatch. In the mornings, I usually throw a gray RSII under an indicator in an attempt to stay ahead of the female hatch. I always keep an eye on the mating swarms to see just how low to the water they are getting. As they get to be about head high, I then switch my tactics a bit. At this point, I usually switch the RSII to a drowned Trico pattern, remove the weight, and fish the rig skinny. In short order, as the Trico columns drop and the insects begin to die, the fish begin to slurp the spents on the surface. Again, I'm staying ahead of the hatch—not by fishing spents on the surface, but by taking advantage of the fishes' position in the water column and what they are looking for. A drowned pattern and a spent pattern nymphed skinny rarely leave me fishless.

You can learn a lot about mayfly hatches by fly fishing a few Trico hatches. As you fish through this hatch, you begin to learn not only the phases of the hatch, but how critical your timing is in deciding what fly you throw into what column, and when and how to fish it. Again, strive to stay ahead of the hatch, and be open to experimentation.

You can use the nymphs I listed above to mimic the clinging, burrowing, or crawling nymphs of this group, but I prefer to use flies that better match the Tricos' color and profile. Fishing a couple different stages at one time is effective. Some of my favorites include:

- Dorsey's Mercury Pheasant Tail and Mercury PMD
- Barr's Beadhead PMD
- Copper John
- Beadhead Red Pheasant Tail
- Beadhead Bubbleback PMD
- Rainbow Warrior
- Craven's Ju Ju PMD
- Beadhead Prince Nymph
- Black, gray, olive RSII (small sizes for Tricos)
- Trico Emerger (black or olive)
- Drowned Trico (black)

If you ask 20 different nymph fishers their 20 favorite flies, you will get 20 different answers. The bugs I've listed work for me, and I fish them with confidence, which is key. Most, if not all, accomplished fly fishers I know have a stable of go-to flies they use to match certain hatches. Once you find a certain level of confidence in a fly pattern, it finds a front row seat in your fly box.

Most folks have heard the old adage that on dark, cloudy days, fish dark bugs, and on clear, sunny days, fish light-colored bugs. I think there is some merit to that old adage, but I tend to focus more on fly contrast than color. On darker days I do go to bugs that are darker in color with more color contrast, more flash, and different color beads, which I think makes the flies easier for the fish to see and mimics the air bubble that insects use to assist their emergence to the surface. On clear, sunny days I fish bugs that have less contrast and more muted tones.

Stoneflies

Another insect that goes through incomplete metamorphosis, or has a nymph stage, is the stonefly (Plecoptera). Because I am from Arizona, stoneflies remind me of scorpions. I still get the willies when I flip a rock and a big stonie points its forked tail up in the air like a scorpion ready to sting. Stoneflies are subsurface predators that can live up to four years underwater and up to two weeks as adults. They go through a series of molts (12 to 33) as nymphs as they grow to maturity and have a distinct split or forked tail.

The stonefly emergence occurs as the bug climbs out of the water to hatch. It's easy to see if there has been a stonefly hatch because dried exoskeletons litter protruding rocks, logs, or the shoreline. That's an easy way to get a fix on the size of the stonefly nymph you are dealing with. Stoneflies inhabit clean, cool, oxygenated water and are good trout food year-round. Clean, cool, oxygenated water? Yup, you'll find plenty of stoneflies in or below riffle sections on the river. Because of their big, clumsy nymph bodies, stoneflies don't swim, but tumble through the current. Now add where they like to live with how they tumble through water, and they become easy pickings for hungry trout.

You can see on the hatch chart that different stoneflies hatch at different times. Luckily these stoneflies are of various sizes and colors, so it is easy to match the nymph with a fly. Don't be fooled: trout eat them through all seasons, and incidentally, I fish them through the winter with great success. Simply flip a few rocks or seine to find the size of the stoneflies in your river if no exoskeletons are present.

Learn to recognize a stonefly adult, and if you observe any fluttering through the air or skittering across the water surface, tie on the nymph to match the adult size. These are some of my favorite stonefly nymph patterns.

GOLDEN STONE

- Pat's Rubberleg
- Barr's Tungstone
- Befus's Wired Stone
- Kaufman's Stone

YELLOW SALLY STONE

- Mercer's Poxyback Little Yellow Stonefly
- Little Sloan
- Iron Sally
- Beadhead Prince Nymph

LITTLE BROWN STONE

- Beadhead Prince Nymph
- Black Copper John

MOLTED GOLDEN STONE

- Mercer's Poxyback Golden Stone

Caddis

The next important insect we will look at is the caddis. Caddis, or Trichoptera, are underwater architects. The larvae build nets, cases, stick or pebble structures, or other types of dwellings using silk. Some caddis are free living, meaning they don't build a structure to live in but spend their underwater life moving freely subsurface. Caddis progress through complete metamorphosis. They begin as eggs, become larvae, pupate into adults, mate, and eventually fall spent to the water. We are mainly concerned with the larva and pupa stages, but some caddis egglaying behavior puts them right back into the water as adults, returning them back to our part of the nymphing realm, so it's good to know the life stages of the caddis.

A trout feeding on caddis pupa as it rises through the columns.

The larva spends most of its life in a protective case. When they are removed from their case, they are basically defenseless, because they are not built to swim. Fish readily eat caddis larva and even caddis within the case year-round. The larva pupates and swims to the surface as a pupa, and when it hits the water surface, it will typically flutter away quickly to the safety of the air. Trout focus on caddis pupae as they swim to the surface, and because the caddis are zipping to the surface, vicious strikes are not uncommon.

When I see the beginnings of a caddis hatch, I make sure I have a caddis pupa imitation on board. (Refer to the hatch chart on pages 126 to 127 to identify times and types of hatching caddis.) I fish the drift in a couple different ways to take advantage of how fish eat the emerging pupae. One way is to dead-drift the bugs through the drift, and at the end of your drift, before the flies rise up through the water columns, simply lift your rod tip, pulling the pupa up through the columns. This imitates a defenseless pupa struggling to get to the surface to escape as an adult.

Another way to fish this pupa stage is to stop the drift about three-quarters of the way by stopping your fly rod swing and allowing the caddis pupa to swing down below you. Once the drift swing is complete, allow the fly to hang below you in the current for a few seconds before you slowly elevate your rod tip for the next cast. Both methods can be deadly. If you see a fish, you can set up above it and forcibly swing your flies up and through the water columns in front of the target fish. Now that's good, clean fun.

Caddis larva or cased caddis is another good winter fly to employ when the fish are not on midges. I often see fish caught on a caddis larva in the winter that have worn the skin off of their lower jaw from rummaging through the rocks. I believe they are looking for caddis or stoneflies to eat.

Toward the end of a caddis hatch, you can begin to pick fish up on female egg-laying caddis that are diving back into the water to deposit eggs. My favorite fly in this situation is a Soft-Hackled Pheasant Tail because it looks like a caddis swimming through the columns. Again, this is a good time to use the swing techniques. The bonus on fishing a caddis pupa is the more action you impart on it, the better it can fish.

Here are some of my favorite caddis larvae and pupae:

LARVAE

- Cased Caddis
- Buckskin
- Rubberleg Chartreuse Copper John
- Peeking Caddis
- Glassy Caddis Larva

PUPAE

- Breadcrust
- LaFontaine's Sparkle Caddis Pupa

- Barr's Graphic Caddis
- Kingrey's Ice Caddis
- Soft-Hackled Pheasant Tail (Beadhead option)
- Soft-Hackled Hares' Ear (Beadhead option)

EGG LAYERS

- Kingrey's Egg-Laying Caddis (I know it's a dry fly . . . trust me, swing it.)
- Silvey's Diving Caddis

Midges

Last and certainly not least, let's look at midges. There are thousands of species, and they progress through the same stages as caddis: larva, pupa, adult, spent. They hatch year-round. You can identify midge adults easily because they look like mosquitoes. It's easy to find midges

This fish ate the Black Beauty midge larva.

on most rivers anywhere from a size 18 to a 26 and smaller. Every fly box should have a good supply and mix of midge larvae and pupae.

Midges, or Chironomidae, are the big little bugs of the insect world. They are a staple in a fish's diet because they are so prolific. Most people think of midges as mainly a winter food for trout, but I have found that fish eat them year-round. When ready to hatch, the pupae rise through the water column only to get stuck in the surface film as they try to emerge as adults. Throughout that entire journey, the little bug is vulnerable to hungry fish.

Don't leave home without midge larvae and pupae in your stable. I keep several colors of the same patterns in my fly box; my favorite colors are black, cream, olive, and red.

LARVAE

- Dorsey's Mercury Flashback Black Beauty
- Rojo Midge
- Bob Dye's Pearl Jam
- Barr's Pure Midge Larva
- Brassie
- Zebra Midge

PUPAE

- Cannon's Snowshoe Midge Emerger
- Dorsey's Top Secret
- Uba's South Platte Shimmer
- Craven's Ju Ju Bee Midge
- Black Mamba Midge Pupa

The Black Mamba

Biological Drift

When fishing a midge larva and pupa rig, I tie my midge larva as my dropper and my midge pupa as the point fly. The larva is typically in the lower column, and the pupa is typically higher, so this is an effective way to align this type of rig. In most cases I fish weight under my indicator followed by the dropper and point flies. The weight bounces on the bottom, and the dropper and point flies ride up above the weight.

When fishing through a PMD hatch, I'll throw a three-bug rig (where that type of rig is legal) consisting of an attractor fly like a San Juan Worm followed by a size 16 Pheasant Tail as the nymph, trailed by a Barr's PMD Emerger. Again, if rigged and fished properly, all three flies should be in the proper columns to match the nymph and emerger phases.

It's counterintuitive, but the fly closest to the weight, when the weight is ticking bottom, will generally be lower in the column than the point fly that is farther away from the weight. If you're drifting two weighted flies, like a stonefly nymph and a Beadhead Prince, this rule doesn't typically apply.

Sometimes, if I want to get my point fly higher into the upper column, I will run up to 18 inches between my dropper and my point fly. Be careful not to go over about 18 inches because you can start missing fish that eat because of the large amount of line below the indicator.

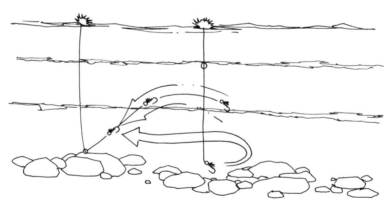

In this example, you can see how method 1 (on the left) can be more accurate in getting proper depth while putting the proper insect stages in the proper columns. In deeper water when fish are feeding in the upper and middle columns I will sometimes use method 2 (on the right). When fish are film-feeding, I'll use a skinny rig.

Use this adjustment anytime you're trying to put nymphs or emergers in the proper columns to match where the fish are feeding.

The more versatile you are, the more fish you'll put in the bag. If I see fish porpoising in the film during a mayfly hatch, unless the fish are eating my nymph rig consistently, I use a dry-dropper or skinny rig to fish the film. For the dry-drop, simply tie on a dry fly, something that closely matches the adults, add 18 to 24 inches of 6X tippet off of the bend of the hook, and tie on an emerger to match what the fish are eating. I then grease the tippet with floatant from the dry fly to about 3 inches from the point fly. This will allow the emerger to hang in the film. You use your dry fly as an indicator, setting on the splash or the swirl.

The Mini-Rig

Another way to take advantage of fishing the surface and various columns at the same time is the mini-rig. I didn't invent it or name it, but I've been using it for years to catch fish that are suspended from the middle column up to the surface film and are feeding on everything from insect adults, to pupae, to emergers. It capitalizes on the dry-dropper method but is a bit different.

I like to use a large, hardy floating dry as the attractor. This first fly is critical to the mini-rig, in that it needs to float all day, be large enough to serve as an indicator and support the weight of two droppers, *and* be able to catch fish. Bugs that have foam bodies and large hair wings like Amy's Ants, Fuzzy Wuzzies, and Foamulators, are my first choice. These flies can mimic anything from stonefly adults to terrestrials.

If the fish eats one of the two droppers below, the dry fly makes a great indicator fly; you set on it just as you would a nymph. If the fish decides to eat the top dry attractor, then you need to set against the fish. For example, if the fish eats your bug going downstream, you need to lift upstream. If the fish eats moving away from you in any way, you set or lift in the opposite direction. I always need to remind clients who have been catching fish under the large attractor to lift on the set if a fish should happen to eat the attractor. If you use a strict nymph set here, odds are the fish will snap off because of the lack of resistance from the line, weight, and indicator on the nymph rig.

The mini-rig uses two flies below the indicator fly. I usually tie my first dropper on a minimum of 30 inches of tippet off of the bend of the big dry fly. I like to use fluorocarbon tippet because it sinks a bit faster than monofilament, which helps get the droppers down quickly.

Usually the first dropper is the pupating or emerging phase of what bugs are coming off. My favorite mini-rig consists of a Beadhead Soft-Hackled Pheasant Tail in the dropper position, acting as a caddis pupa or female caddis diving to lay eggs. My point fly is about 10 inches from the dropper. I tie off of the eye of the dropper when I drop down to the point fly. This eye-to-eye connection helps create a swimming look to that bug. My point or last fly can be another pupa or emerger. Typically I like to run a *Baetis* emerger here, such as an RSII, and if I am fishing unweighted droppers, I put a number six split shot exactly between the dropper and the point flies.

This rig can be easily customized to hit different columns with different stages of insects to match where and what fish are eating. Some folks raise an eyebrow when I tie 30 inches of tippet to the first fly, thinking it's much too long to be effective, but I have found this amount of tippet works perfectly fine water of any depth where fish are suspended in the columns looking for food. When fishing shallow water, fast water, deep water, slow water, or any other kind of water, the key, as always, is the setup and cast angles.

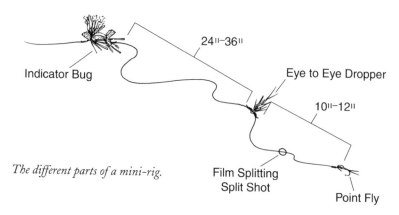

Indicator Bug

24"–36"

Eye to Eye Dropper

10"–12"

The different parts of a mini-rig.

Film Splitting
Split Shot

Point Fly

Other Bugs in the Box

There are other flies that, although not part of the big four (caddis, stoneflies, midges, and mayflies), should inhabit your fly box. You should always have a good supply of other options that you can drift under yarn. Some of my most successful flies don't emerge or pupate, but they get the job done. I have included several of these bugs on the hatch chart. Egg flies are probably the most effective attractor pattern I throw, and they are especially good in spring and fall due to spawning. Please don't fish to trout on their redds or spawning beds. Those fish need to be left alone to do their thing. Fish to the ones below the spawning beds that are eagerly awaiting a free meal of eggs or a leech chasing an egg. In the spring, I fish for brown trout eating eggs, and in the fall, rainbows. Be careful not to walk on spawning beds if you're wading.

Egg flies work year-round on several tailwaters I fish because of the constant cool water tailwaters provide. Worm, crane fly, and scud patterns work anytime, but can be especially effective during runoff, or murky water conditions, because these creatures are dislodged by the rushing water and tumble helplessly to eager trout.

I commonly run a streamer or leech pattern dead-drifted under an indicator as an attractor fly. Another way to use a leech is to tie it as a point fly about 3 inches below an egg pattern. Simply dead-drift them, or fish them the same as you would a caddis pupa to elicit impressive strikes. Those methods work well year-round but especially during spawn.

There are several egg patterns out there, so find the ones that match the color and size of egg the fish are laying. My go-to egg pattern is the peach Flash Tail Egg, with the Nuclear Egg a close second. As for leeches, I like a size 14 Squirrel Tail Leech or size 12 to 14 olive Slump Buster.

Sometimes you can dial right into what fish are eating, but at other times, well, they are simply amusing. This winter I was guiding two clients during a windy snowstorm. We eased up into a riffle that holds fish, armed with a nymph rig consisting of a size 12 Mercer's Stone and a blue midge larva. On the first drift, a nice rainbow came up and ate

Hatch Chart

BUGS	JAN	FEB	MAR	APR	MAY	JUN	JUL	AUG	SEP	OCT	NOV	DEC
MAYFLIES												
BWO			X	X	X	X		/	X	X	X	
PMD						X	X	X	X			
Green Drake							X	X	X			
Blue Quill								X	X	X		
Callibaetis					X	X	X					
Trico							X	X	X	X		
CADDIS												
American Caddis				X	X	/	X	X				
Spotted Caddis					X	X	X	X				
Green Caddis						X	X	X	X	/	/	
Olive Caddis						X	X	X	X			
STONEFLIES												
Golden Stone				X	X	X	X	X	X	/		
Yellow Sally							X	X	X	X		
Little Brown			/	X	X	X	X					

(continued)

Hatch Chart

BUGS	JAN	FEB	MAR	APR	MAY	JUN	JUL	AUG	SEP	OCT	NOV	DEC
MIDGES												
Black Midge	X	X	X	X	X	X	X	X	X	X	X	
Gray Midge	X	X	X	X	X	X	X	X	X	X	X	
Olive Midge	X	X	X	X	X	X	X	X	X	X	X	
TERRESTRIALS												
Ants						X	X	X	X	X	/	
Beetles						X	X	X	X	/		
Hoppers							X	X	X	/		
Worms	X	X	X	X	X	X	X	X	X	X	X	
OTHERS												
Streamers	X	X	X	X	X	X	X	X	X	X	X	
Egg Fly				X	X	X	X	X	X	X	X	

This hatch chart represents typical hatch times in the Rocky Mountain Region. Other regions vary.

the yarn indicator. That fish took it under and actually made a short run with it. After the indicator popped to the surface, one of my clients asked, "Now, why did he do that?" To which I replied, "Because he doesn't have hands."

Sometimes you can match the fly profile, size, and color perfectly, and instead fish will eat something out of the ordinary. That does not dilute the fact that when you marry entomology to all you know about reading water, reading fish, basic nymph rigging, and the drift, you will begin to consistently put fish in the bag. A good working knowledge of entomology will complete anyone's playbook.

Xs and Os

- Understand how entomology is married to the basic tenets of the playbook.
- Learn the basic stages of mayflies, stoneflies, caddis, and midges.
- Learn how to decipher what fish are feeding on by working backward from the adult, flipping rocks, seining, or pumping fish.
- Understand a biological drift.
- Learn to fish in different columns by adjusting tippet lengths.

11

Flingin' and Bringin'

The fly rod acts as a third-class lever. It's basically an extension of your arm. I envision it as one piece from my elbow to the rod tip. I apply force to the lever or fly rod during the cast; the fly rod, in turn, loads or stores the potential energy; and when I stop the fly rod, the energy is transferred to the fly line. Remember middle school physics and the Law of Conservation of Energy? Energy is neither created nor destroyed; it only changes forms. When casting, the fly rod transfers the energy, and when landing fish, the fly rod absorbs the energy. The rod absorbs the mass and velocity of the fish as you provide the correct angles to absorb the maximum forces to prevent the leader and tippet from snapping. The actions of casting and landing fish mirror one another. It all comes down to your expertise in handling the fly rod.

The Grip

Casting begins with your grip. Grip the fly rod as you would grip the handle of a briefcase. Hold the rod grip in your fingers; don't shove it back into your palm. When I am teaching beginners how to grip, I'll ask them to hold their hand out as if to shake my hand, and I place the rod in their fingers and adjust their thumb to the top of the grip.

Proper and consistent rod grip is important for accuracy, distance, and fly fishing comfort.

Some folks like to place their index finger on the top of the grip, but I like to use the thumb because it automatically lines up the knuckles of my fingers and puts me in position for the next step. Also, when using your thumb on top of the grip, it frees up your index finger. I've discussed this previously, but it's worth repeating that the index finger is best used for controlling the management loop during the drift and "pinching cork" during the set. I've tried to use the index finger on top of the grip, but to me, it's plain uncomfortable, and leaves me wanting for more line control. Whichever method you choose, just make sure you line up the thumb or index finger with the rod spine directly on top of, or opposite, the guides of the rod.

The next concept is to use a knuckles-first approach to casting and landing fish. This is a critical component and should not be overlooked. Imagine knocking on a door with the fly rod grip in your hand. This hand placement is the basis for what we do from here on out because it sets up the proper angle between the rod butt and wrist. The angle created between the rod butt and wrist is important, and it is fundamental to the cast.

I tell beginners not to change the angle between the wrist and rod butt. It's much more efficient and effective for beginners to cast with a solid, static wrist. Plenty of intermediate fly casters have issues, which I'll describe more in detail later, because they lose the rod-to-wrist relationship, or they break the angle by bending their wrist. Advanced fly casters have mastered how to use the wrist angles during the cast.

Roll Casting

Now that we have the proper grip, let's break down the casting mechanics. We are going to begin with a simple roll cast. Snip off any flies on your rig. You can tie a bit of yarn to any leader left if you desire. With the proper grip and rod butt to wrist alignment secure (refer back to the rod grip illustration on page 61), flip out about 15 feet of fly line from the rod tip, then capture the fly line between your index or trigger finger and the rod grip, holding an 18-inch loop behind it. Let this

Notice the D formed behind the fly rod.

management loop dangle as you tuck your casting elbow into a slot comfortably next to your side.

Provided you have the rod butt angle locked in, your elbow simply acts as the fulcrum for the fly rod and can comfortably stay locked in position during the roll cast. It may travel forward and down a bit during the roll cast, but should always stay on the same plane. If your wrist is secure and your elbow stays on the same plane as it travels forward, your rod tip can only do the same. The rod tip must travel in the same flat plane as your elbow to ensure that you are loading the fly rod properly. I notice many intermediate casters struggling here as they lose the rod-to-wrist relationship; this causes them to also lose the fly rod load.

Proper body and rod alignment creates a loaded fly rod ready for the roll cast.

The rod tip must follow a flat plane. Each component relies on the other to provide proper fly rod loading. As you learn to secure the wrist and follow the proper casting plane, the rod will begin to load properly. This is also the basis for other casting techniques, so master it. Remember, no arcs allowed.

Now bring your rod tip up. Imagine two clock faces: one in front of you and one to your fly rod side. Point the rod tip at the one o'clock position on the clock in front of you, and do the same to the clock to your rod side. Now you should be able to see a fly line loop forming from your rod tip to your feet. That D loop loads your fly rod.

At this point, pick out an object, such as a leaf or piece of grass, and concentrate on keeping everything secure. Cast the rod to three o'clock on the fly rod side clock, while pointing your thumb at your target. I call this "thumbing the rod tip" because the rod tip will travel the same path as your thumb. If your thumb travels off the horizontal or vertical planes, so will your rod tip. Keep repeating the cast, and if you notice the line is not laying all the way out for you, then you are probably breaking the angle between the rod butt and your wrist, or you're not forming a good D loop. Inspect your position, tighten it up, and keep trying.

When you are roll casting in the river, the D loop can be somewhat modified by the current. Instead of a classic D loop, you get an elongated loop as the water pulls your fly line downstream. This is fine because what you lose in a classic D-loop rod load, you gain in the force of the water pulling on your fly line. (The current helps load the rod.) After the position set (see page 72) and as you raise your rod tip to prepare to roll cast, pick up slowly and methodically as you choose your next target. This lets the force of the water load the rod, allowing you to effortlessly roll cast to your next target.

Casting is about tempo, even roll casting, and it should become part of your drift. I always tell folks that if I can hear your fly rod whipping through the air, you're working too hard and not allowing the rod to properly load. Think how well roll casting is set up after a position set, as you smoothly bring your fly rod tip to the one o'clock position. It will become one fluid motion and become one with the drift. Tempo, tempo, tempo. I see many intermediate and advanced fly fishers who need to polish and simplify their roll casting. Bad habits form easily. Once you truly master the roll cast, forehand and backhand, you can nymph anywhere.

Full Cast

The key to the full cast is to let the fly rod do the work, maintain fluidity, and keep the fly rod on consistent paths through casting planes. If you have a good grasp on the roll cast, you're nearly halfway there. Instead of forming a D loop to load the rod, you backcast. The backcast adds more movement to your cast, so you need to lock in your casting elbow, grip, and the angle of the rod butt to your wrist.

If you are a beginner, or you're having trouble with your casting, I suggest you keep your elbow on a flat plane throughout the cast. Some anglers run their elbow along a flat plane, while others run their elbow on that same plane but add an up and down motion. Folks usually have trouble with the full cast when they break their wrists, create an arc in their casting, or have improper tempo or timing.

Imagine your elbow is on a tabletop, and keep it on that flat plane. As you cast forward and back, your elbow travels along the top of the table. Where your elbow goes, your thumb follows, and so does your rod tip. This is a great way to begin to full cast and a great way to troubleshoot your casting at any stage of your evolution. Advanced casters have mastered the art of moving their elbow back *and* up as they backcast, while maintaining a flat rod tip path. Both methods are fine; just find what works best for you.

Begin full casting by setting up the same way you did for roll casting. Throw a roll cast out in front of you, making sure there is no slack in your fly line from the tip of your rod. With your fly rod tip at three o'clock, begin to accelerate the rod tip up and back to the one o'clock position and stop. Your fly line should be behind you at this point, your elbow at your side, your thumb about hat high, and your fly rod tip at about the one o'clock position. Pause here and check to see if that is where you stopped. Now, sitting at the one o'clock position, cast forward as you did when roll casting, and stop the rod tip at three o'clock.

The way you accelerate the backcast to a stop is important; it should be a gradual acceleration until you near the top of the cast where it increases markedly just before you pause. This allows you to begin to build velocity and load the fly rod.

Now it's time to put the entire cast together. This time, when you backcast, accelerate from the three o'clock position, pause at the one o'clock position, wait for an instant, and then cast forward.

Do this several times while watching the loop that forms and feeling for a slight tug at the top of your backcast as your fly line loads your

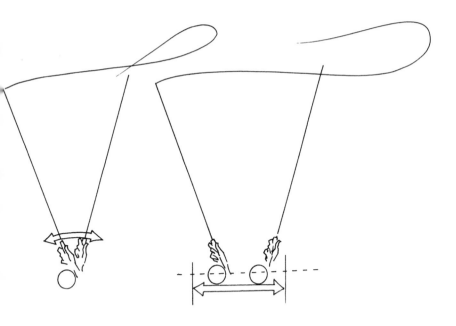

Through the casting stroke, the tip of the fly rod should remain on a straight path and a flat plane. Concentrate on the proper grip and the angle between the rod butt and wrist. The rod tip will generally match your thumb cast plane.

fly rod. As you practice, look at the path your elbow travels, your wrist alignment, and the loop that's formed. Once you're comfortable with the tempo of the cast, it's time to focus on the rod tip as you cast. You want your rod tip to travel in a straight line on a flat plane. This will give you a nice loop and use all of the physical advantages the fly rod can give you.

Here's where I'd like to touch on the angle between your wrist and rod butt again. A tailing loop, or a loop where the upper portion dips down below the lower portion, is typically caused by breaking your wrist, poor tempo, or failing to cast in a straight line on a flat plane. By breaking your wrist, you neglect to load the fly rod, among other things, which in turn helps form a tailing loop. Tailing loops kill casting accuracy, distance, and ease. I advise beginners and intermediate fly casters who are having problems to inspect rod-wrist alignment initially. Once you determine that the wrist-rod butt angle is secure, begin to troubleshoot the other factors that cause tailing loops.

I have had the pleasure to guide and fish with advanced fly casters. These folks all had different mechanics but could cast with ease, distance, and accuracy. Although they arrived to that point differently, what I observed was they all had a perfect rod tip path and they also moved their wrists during the cast stroke. For shorter casting and roll casting, advanced fly casters maintain a tight angle between the wrist and the rod, but as they begin to reach for distance, the wrist becomes a player in the cast. The longer the cast, the more the fly rod lays back behind them (all the way to three o'clock) and the more the wrist opens up. Although the wrist opens up in the backcast, as they begin the forward stroke, the wrist once again quickly attains the proper alignment, enabling them to efficiently lay out line.

Like any physical pursuit, it's all about practice. Quarterbacks work on throwing motion in virtually every practice session because it's the foundation of their position. The roll cast, in my opinion, is the foundation of a good cast. Factor in tempo, acceleration, and solid mechanics, and you can become more than proficient quickly. It's never a bad idea to videotape yourself, pick up a casting video, or find a qualified caster to give you a hand.

Hauling

A haul is a movement by the hand that holds your fly line (your off-rod hand) that adds additional load to the fly rod. All you're doing is accelerating the fly line by pulling downward during the power stroke of the cast. The power stroke of a cast can be either the fore- or backcast. It's when the fly rod is under optimum load as you prepare to cast. Often, when nymphing, you can insert a single haul into the forward/power stroke of the roll cast or full cast to help move heavier rigs and cut through the wind. Because I typically don't use long casts during nymphing, I don't feel the need to double-haul, or add a haul on the backcast under normal conditions. However, I have sometimes used both a single and double haul while nymphing to combat high winds or to make longer casts.

The key to hauling starts with making sure you remove all slack before you backcast. Beginning with your rod hand and off-rod hand close together, accelerate smoothly into your backcast while pulling the fly line downward toward your off-hip pocket. As you reach the top of your backcast and come to a pause, bring your off-grip hand back up toward the reel, feeding line to the backcast and repositioning your hands in preparation for the forward cast. Next, as you begin casting forward, and your hands are close together, haul again to further power and accelerate the line.

In short, you add a haul to the backcast, reposition your hands while feeding line, and add another haul to the forward cast. Once you have the double haul mastered, the single haul for a roll cast becomes second nature. Simply set the rod position in preparation of the cast as outlined earlier and, using your off-rod hand, accelerate the fly line with a downward pull during the cast. Sometimes, the D loop can't load the fly rod as much as you may need to execute a longer roll cast or if you're casting into the teeth of a high wind. Knowing how to properly single- and double-haul can add to your nymphing strategies and give you another skill set for your playbook. There is a ton of information out there dealing with hauling. Again, find what works best for you.

Specialty Casts

Remember when you're casting a nymph rig that you have an indicator, flies, and a weight on your rig. Slow down your tempo a bit more to open up your loop, because all of those gizmos create hinges in your leader. This will reduce dreaded wind knots, which can bench you for a while as you clean them up. As I mentioned earlier, you can nymph-fish anywhere by simple roll casting. When I nymph, most of my casts are simple flips or roll casts. I do, however, use a reach mend and S mend on nearly every cast, whether it's a full cast or roll cast.

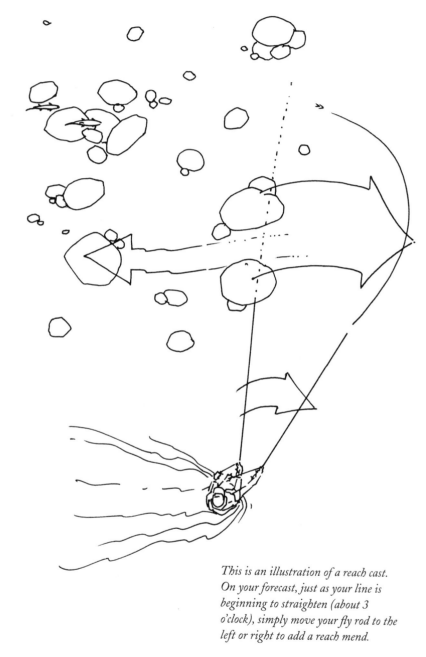

This is an illustration of a reach cast. On your forecast, just as your line is beginning to straighten (about 3 o'clock), simply move your fly rod to the left or right to add a reach mend.

The reach cast is easy to master, and all it's designed to do is add a mend into your cast before it hits the water. This allows you to fish the initial stages without having to immediately mend when your bugs hit the water. The less you have to mend while maintaining a good drift, the better, so you aren't caught mending when a fish eats.

When you cast forward, as your line straightens out in front of you, and before your flies hit the water, move your rod to the right or left to add a mend. It takes a bit of practice, but if you have solid casting fundamentals, it should be a piece of cake.

I also frequently add an S mend to the roll or full cast—it's like putting a shock absorber in the fly line before it hits the water. The S mend is effective for longer casts, but it proves helpful for short work as well. It consists of several S-shaped mends in the line before it hits the water. This can be a huge advantage, especially when throwing longer line, because it reduces the need for huge upstream mends that are not only difficult but detract from your ability to set quickly.

Simply roll cast, and as your fly rod begins to flatten out over the water abruptly stop it parallel to the water and force several flat, back-and-forth actions to the rod tip.

Grab a pencil and hold it like you would your rod handle. Mimic a roll cast, stop with the pencil flat to the floor, and quickly add four or five back-and-forth motions. Each motion should be about six inches back and forth to start with, and as you go from a pencil to the fly rod, the distance of the cast will determine the amount of distance to move back and forth.

While the S mend is equally terrific for shorter and longer nymphing work, the tuck cast is typically used for closer applications. I use the tuck cast when I need to get the flies through the surface film and down quickly into the column. One application is where you are fishing a shelf into a pool. Sometimes, because of the drift characteristics, it's tough to both get over the shelf and into the head of the pool. In most instances this forces you to not only add more weight in an attempt to get the rig down, but to cast farther upstream to get the bugs down to where they need to be as you fish over the shelf. Both adjustments lead you to continually snag above the shelf section. Use the tuck cast to solve that problem.

The tuck cast, if done properly, gets bugs down quickly as it forces the flies through the film. This negates the need for a bunch of additional weight and the need to cast farther upstream. It's simple to perform. Again, you need to set up with the proper mechanics, so grab that pencil again to mimic your rod handle. Roll cast forward as you usually would, but this time abruptly stop the pencil at shoulder level, at about the two o'clock position. Most people stop here thinking this is enough for a tuck cast, but you're not done yet. After stopping at the two o'clock position, without lowering the pencil, flex your wrist down until the pencil is parallel to the floor. As you lay the pencil flat, you'll notice your elbow, wrist, and hand move up. That's perfect. Remember, you first stop abruptly with the fly rod at two o'clock and your hand is shoulder high. Only after that do you flatten the fly rod to parallel.

Fighting and Landing Fish

Fighting and landing fish use all of the same physics that casting does. You use the flex of the lever, or fly rod, to absorb or load the rod in an effort to reduce pressure on small-diameter leaders and tippets. The more mechanical advantage you can achieve, the better your chances of landing the fish. My goal is to not only land every fish I hook, but it is to do it quickly and efficiently. It's all about leverage and angles.

Once you set on and hook up a fish, bring your rod tip up and away as you spool in the slack from your management loop. Most reels have a neat feature that allows you to simply spin the line spool with your free hand. This is called "spooling." I constantly tell clients to get that fly reel up. That usually falls on deaf ears, so lately I have been saying, "Point your rod elbow at the fish!" For some reason that clicks, and it puts the fly rod in a position to use its flex efficiently. I like to see the rod elbow pointed at the fish, and the rod thumb at least as high as the hat brim. This position takes pounds of pressure at the reel and reduces it to ounces of pressure at the tippet because of the rod height or leverage.

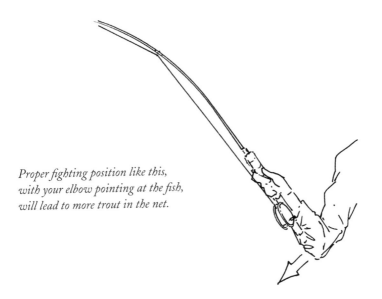

Proper fighting position like this,
with your elbow pointing at the fish,
will lead to more trout in the net.

Notice that I focus on the position of the fly reel; it's not all about getting the rod tip up. Sure, most of the time you will be fine if you just get the rod tip up, but I believe that alone puts you in a defensive mode. You need to be on the offensive as much as you can when fighting and landing a fish. Point the rod elbow at the fish, and position the fly rod anywhere you need to keep proper pressure on the fish.

After you get the rod in position, it's important to get the fish on the reel. There's thousands of hours of technology in those drag systems, so put it to use. If you've done your homework, and set your drag properly, you shouldn't have to make any adjustments. Just spool up the slack, let go of the fly line, and begin to use strategies to land that fish. Again, let go of the fly line, and let the reel do its job.

Most beginners clamp down on the fly line at the cork when the fish makes its first run or headshake. This leads to a lot of fish coming unbuttoned. Another common mistake I see at hookup is folks have a tendency to set and point the rod skyward while backing up. At this point I exclaim, "Keep your feet—don't move back!" Stepping back simply multiplies the pressure to your light tippets, and I see most snap-offs here. I often wonder where they think they are going? Resist the urge.

Most fish make about three runs: one at hookup, one somewhere in midfight, and one more when they see my net or ugly mug. Anticipate these runs by keeping your form and going to the reel in short, quick bursts. I call it the machine-gun approach. Do short, quick reeling when the fish gives you the chance, followed by a break to see what the fish is doing. In this way, you shouldn't be caught reeling when the fish decides to make a run or headshake, and you will be prepared to quickly reel when a fish swims toward you.

I have listened to good friend and Blue Quill Angler guide J. Core walk people through landing big fish. He always talks about getting the advantage from the fish by smoothly applying pressure in the direction you want the fish to move. He explains to clients how during the fight the fish has the advantage in the faster water, and if you ease it this way or that, you'll gain the advantage back. It's like listening to a blow-by-blow account at a boxing match. I've seen him walk beginners through the process of fighting big fish many times. What he is doing is teaching folks to patiently "feel" the fish through the fly rod, how to apply smooth constant pressure, and how to gain the advantage when you "feel" the opportunity. He's good at it.

You need to get the advantage over fish without muscling them. There's a fine line between muscling or horsing a fish and applying smooth, constant pressure. What none of us want to see is a fish breaking off with hardware in its mouth. To get and keep the advantage you have to use angles. Use the leverage you have to smoothly move that fish to a position where you can eventually land it. It's not unusual to have to move upstream or downstream to maintain the mechanical advantage.

I like to coach people to attempt to keep a 90-degree angle between the fly rod and the fish. Most often, this is not entirely possible, but it gets the point across to try to keep side leverage at all times. We are going to lose most of the fish that get downstream of us and begin to gator roll on the surface if we maintain a high rod tip that's

Zack Waltz applies mechanical advantage to smoothly land a South Platte River trout.

pointing straight up throughout the fight. That's why I teach clients to keep the elbow pointed at the fish and to be ready to lay the fly rod parallel to the water if need be. If the fish begins to gator roll, simply lay your fly rod flat to the water (bankside) to regain the upper hand. You and the fish become married at hookup. It's give and take, and it's a dance. Don't be that guy who is slowly swaying as his partner is jamming to the music! Match the movement, and stay on the offensive.

On bigger fish, if you begin to tire, you can take a quick break by sliding your off-rod hand up the fly rod about 5 inches from the junction of the rod and grip. This changes the fulcrum point and allows your rod arm to rest. If the fish decides to run, quickly move your hand back to regain your mechanical advantage. Again, folks get into trouble when they allow a fish to get directly downstream and roll on the surface. That rarely ends well. It's not unusual to have to extend your rod

Briefly changing the fulcrum point while fighting large fish can give you a huge advantage.

arm forward and flat toward the bank while creating at least a 45-degree angle between the fish and the fly rod. Then, as the fish stops rolling on the surface, you once again get that rod tip in position to make the next countermove.

Another problem area is when a bigger fish makes a run. People have a tendency to freeze up, and the reel can't keep up with the fish. On really big, strong fish in fast or high water, point your fly rod at the fish and let it go. When it's done running, get the rod back up, and reel up any slack that may have formed. When a fish jumps, bow to it. In other words, lower your rod tip to give the fish some slack. When a fish jumps, because there is usually line still underwater, it exerts pressure on your leader and tippet. Simply bow, and as the fish reenters the water, get the tension back on it by lifting the rod tip.

Most big fish are lost in the first few seconds after hookup. Plenty of folks freeze, or clamp down on the rod handle and fly line, and that's a recipe for disaster. There's another factor at play here that few talk about, but I see it all the time. Experienced anglers have hooked plenty of bigger fish to know that you don't match how hard the fish is pulling by pulling back. Sounds simple, I know, but I see less experienced anglers do this all the time.

Sometimes fish come unbuttoned unexpectedly and your fly rod will flex the opposite direction and your flies end up behind you in the bushes. If that happens consistently, it means you're pulling equally as hard as the fish. When you do that, many fish either snap off or come unhooked because of huge amounts of pressure on the fish's mouth, the flies, knots, and tippets. Next time a fish comes unbuttoned for no apparent reason, check yourself to see if your flies snapped back unusually hard. You may be putting too much pressure on the fish.

John Leatherman keeps good lateral leverage while hustling downstream to land a large Colorado trout.

Once the fish begins to tire, and you have maneuvered it to water suitable for landing it, you can go to the net. As a side note, I like a rubberized net that protects what protects the fish—their slime. I like to reel all the way in until only about two feet of fly line remains past the tip of the rod. Refrain from reeling your leader into the guides because it can snap. Get the fish's head out of the water, position your net, and begin to slide the fish to you on the water surface.

The last move in the netting process is to take a step toward the fish, extend your fly rod high overhead, get over the fish with the rod tip, and dip the net under the entire fish. You should do this in one smooth motion, but we all know that fish don't always read the script. Lately, we've been catching some fine fish on the South Platte. They're big, strong, healthy fish, and I've been using another method to increase the odds of landing these bigger fish. What I try to do is continually move the client to get into a position where the fish tires 10 to 15 feet directly upstream of us in calmer water. The key here is that the fish is tired and swimming directly away from us upstream. As the client begins to get over the fish, reeling in line, with upward pressure, most fish will simply turn or roll to the pressure right into my waiting net. You don't need to completely tire the fish out to accomplish this; actually it's more desirable to leave some vinegar in them because they zip right into the waiting net. Try it sometime!

Please wet your hands before you handle the fish, and try to unhook it quickly. Hemostats come in handy here, and don't forget to pinch down your fly barbs. Don't worry about knots or tangles at this time that may have formed during landing—just get that fish back into the drink. For smaller fish, I use the same techniques, but instead of going to the net, I simply slide my fingers down the leader, grasp the fly (not the leader), and pluck the fly free, while the fish remains in the water.

With fish that are foul-hooked, it's not unusual for me to rodeo the fish. I call it rodeoing fish because it's not unlike a calf roper running down the rope to throw a calf as the horse holds the line taut. If it's on a client's rig, I quickly move down the fly line to the fish to net it. Fish can run out of oxygen if they are held in a current where they can't get water flow through their gills, so netting and releasing them quickly is important.

Taking pictures is a way to preserve the memory. I like to take pictures over the water, in case the fish doesn't cooperate, and if I should lose my grip, it'll fall into the water. Please don't put fish on rocks, grass, sand, logs, or snow to get a picture; it could damage their protective slime. Cradle the fish as you get a picture, and smile! When you revive a fish, place it upright in softer water—that is usually right below you in your backwash—and give the fish as much time as it needs to kick away from you of its own volition. Keep an eye on it after it kicks away, just to be sure it is fine.

Even though we discussed casting and landing fish, the impetus of this chapter is learning to use the stick. Understanding the mechanics and physics of a fly rod and how to use the information to your advantage is a great addition to your playbook. Arguably, mastery of fly rod physics is the main skill set that leads to success on the river. Casting, fighting and landing fish, and controlling the drift are all functions of the fly rod. Through practice and experience, the fly rod will become an extension of your body (sappy as that sounds), and you will become one with the fly rod.

Xs and Os

- Know the body and rod placement relationships.
- Learn the mechanics and fundamentals of the casts.
- Understand the physics behind a fly rod.
- Learn how to use the fly rod to gain a mechanical advantage over fighting fish as you land them.

12

Closing Thoughts

I have had the opportunity to coach several running backs over the years. I always began with basic agility, ball protection, acceleration, pad levels, and reading the defense. I liked watching the progression a back went through as he gained experience. With skills in place, and a systematic coaching approach, the back would move from running robotically to running while seeing the entire field. He would begin to "feel" the defense and make adjustments before the defense could respond. After the handoff, the running back would make subtle adjustments and change angles on the run. It's a thing of beauty, born of practice that becomes instinct. I look at fly fishing in the same light. You learn and practice the skills systematically until they eventually become instinctual, and you begin to see the entire field.

Recently, I went to see my doctor for my yearly physical. We talked of fly fishing quite a bit, but one thing he said to me struck a chord. Being relatively new to the sport, he went out on a guided trip to a local water. He said that after that experience he realized two things: "Guides know what they're doing, and there isn't any luck involved." Now, I'm not pushing guides, so I'll leave that part of the statement alone, and I agree totally with the second part of that comment. Every now and then, you'll have a fish eat your fly in an improbable way, but the vast majority of the fish hooked by fly fishing do not involve luck.

I have a young German short-haired pointer named Blue. When I got Blue, we already had an established pointer that not only ran the household, but was in charge in the field as well. As I hunted them more and more together, I began to realize how little confidence Blue was displaying. He was always unsure of his nose, and his body language showed it. Confident he knew what to do in the field, I began to hunt him by himself. Blue blossomed into a fine hunting companion after just a few short trips because he found he could do it. Learning the skills is important, but confidence is key. Success leads to confidence, which leads to more confidence. It will come.

Just like the 8-year-old boy who pointed out the ape and iguana on the mountainside, I try to approach each day as a gift. Take it all in. It's so difficult to do that if you're not clear on how you plan to approach the river. This is the main reason I preach about tempo and cadence. The tempo with which you approach the river can make the difference between a good and bad day.

I always try to convey to clients to match the speed and pulse of the river. Not only does nymphing become easier, but the entire game slows down and you can see the entire field. I had a client tell me one day that she never used to see anything but the indicator because she was focused on it solely. She also said it wasn't until she consciously tried to match the rivers' cadence that she began to pick up fish around or in the vicinity of her indicator while setting on the flash of a fish eat. The simple act of relaxing and matching the tempo of the river will help you pick up more fish; plus it makes for a more satisfying experience.

River Etiquette

I would be remiss if I didn't include river etiquette in this book. I see infractions all the time, and I spend a good deal of time discussing river etiquette in my classes. From folks cutting off others or high-holing, to people pinching and boxing you in, it can be a real problem. I break the river into two parts: river right and river left as you look downstream. Depending on the size of the river, you can comfortably fish both sides to the centerline; just don't crowd the other angler or fish directly

Alan Peak works a run with plenty of room.

across the river. If it's a bigger body of water, big enough that on your best day you can't cast to the centerline, then you can fish directly across the river. Just use common sense, and do what your mom always told you: "Treat others as you expect to be treated."

When I approach the river, and see an angler in the run I wish to fish, I always begin with a cordial greeting. If I can see the angler from the road, I'll pass that section and go to another. After the greeting, I always ask which way he or she is headed. After that is established, I'll ask something along the lines of, "Can we fish behind you?" or "How about we give you this entire run, the bend above it, and the next run?"

Not too long ago, I was lead vehicle in a long line of trailing cars. We had a large group fishing with us, and when I led the procession into a parking area two guys hesitantly looked up as they put their waders on. I immediately went up to those guys, introduced myself, and told them not to worry; we would certainly give them first dibs.

You should've seen the relief on their faces, and as it turned out, they were going to hoof it several bends down river and fish their way back. Not only that, we had a brief conversation about what bugs the fish were on, and I gave them a few bugs to try.

Be cordial and give other anglers plenty of river to fish. Every time I've treated folks this way, they respond with "thanks" and a smile. If you do pass someone on the river, get well up on the bank as you walk by the runs he plans to fish. Don't spook any of his fish. My rule of thumb is give them room, a smile, a bend, and a run or two.

Some other points to ponder include knowing the regulations, respecting private property, packing out your trash, pinching barbs on hooks, controlling dogs, and giving the right-of-way to kids. Again, just common sense stuff. I've only had a few instances of folks not keeping their dog in order; honestly, I worry for the critter because I don't want to see it stuck with a fly or hit by a car. If I see an instance where any etiquette rules are broken, I politely use that situation to teach folks.

Well, it's *usually* a polite conversation. I have observed a fair amount of poaching on the South Platte. Unfortunately it's not unusual to see people fishing with bait in prohibited areas, keeping too many fish, or keeping fish outside the slot limits. These conversations are not nearly as pleasant, and I report the incident. Danny Brennan, the guide at Flies and Lies, and other guides and outfitters, do a bang-up job of helping police that river. Those folks could use some help because they can't be everywhere. Please report all incidences you observe, and try to get a license plate number.

Personalize Your Playbook

I've seen different styles of running backs be successful, from power backs, to slashers, to jitter-bugs—they use their strengths to get the job done. In the same way, you can become a good nymph fisher regardless of your style if you adjust your playbook to match your strengths.

If you're a beginning fly fisher, the playbook is designed to not only afford you the basics, but get you to the next level quickly. For intermediate and advanced fly fishermen, the playbook is designed to help you take your game to the next level, to be able to see the entire field. In essence, the playbook is a tool that will help you go to the river, take the same things other folks see, and make succinct adjustments. These adjustments are based on solid fundamentals, a systematic approach, and your personal style, and they will take your game up a full notch. You never punt when you're using the playbook; guesses become options that you choose based on observed evidence of what the defense is giving you.

The playbook is not just something you read. It's something *you* design, develop, and master. From the basic nymph rig to the drift, you are constantly evolving and personalizing your playbook. It is something you own, and it will be as comprehensive as you make it.

The next time you hit the river, I truly hope that you use the strategies I have outlined in this book. It's like preparing for a play-off game; get all of your Xs and Os going in the same direction. Everyone has room for improvement, me included, so keep at it, be diligent, fish with purpose, confidence, tempo, and fear no water. It's in the playbook.

Fly Recipe Appendix

- **BIG NASTY SAN JUAN WORM**
  Originator: Variation of Paul Pacheco original
  Tier: Duane Redford
  Hook: #14-16 Tiemco 9300
  Thread: Pink 6/0 UNI-Thread
  Under body: Dark olive Ice Dub UV
  Abdomen: Worm brown Ultra Chenille

- **BEADHEAD SOFT-HACKLE PHEASANT TAIL**
  Originator: Pacific Fly Company
  Tier: Duane Redford
  Hook: #16-18 Mustad 3906
  Bead: Gold, brass, or tungsten to match
  Thread: Black 8/0 UNI-Thread
  Tail: Pheasant tail fibers
  Abdomen: Pheasant tail fibers
  Rib: Gold Ultra Wire, reverse wrapped
  Collar: Partridge
  Thorax: Peacock herl

- **BRACHY PUPA (CADDIS)**
  Originator: Duane Redford
  Tier: Duane Redford
  Hook: #14-18 Tiemco 2488
  Thread: Olive 8/0 UNI-Thread
  Tail: RSII wing material
  Abdomen: Light olive Ice Dub UV with RSII "bubble"
  Wing: White Antron
  Thorax: Peacock herl

- **GIRL SCOUT**
  Originator: Duane Redford
  Tier: Duane Redford
  Hook: #18-22 Tiemco 2487
  Thread: Dark brown 8/0 UNI-Thread
  Tail: Dun microfibbets
  Abdomen: Dark brown 8/0 UNI-Thread
  Rib: Olive 8/0 UNI-Thread
  Wing: Pearl Flashabou
  Head: Thread, wrapped, with head cement

- **PERIWINKLE**
  Originator: Unknown
  Tier: Duane Redford
  Hook: #18-22 Tiemco 2487
  Bead: Gunmetal (x-small)
  Thread: Olive UTC 70
  Abdomen: Olive UTC 70
  Rib: Black Brassie, reverse wrapped
  Collar: Olive Ice Dub UV

- **BROWN RSII (CHOCOLATE THUNDER)**
  Originator: Solitude Fly Company
  Tier: Duane Redford
  Hook: #18-20 Tiemco 2487
  Thread: Brown 8/0 UNI-Thread
  Tail: Hen hackle fibers
  Abdomen: Brown 8/0 UNI-Thread
  Rib: Gold Ultra Wire, reverse wrapped
  Wing: White Razor Foam
  Head: Thread, wrapped, with head cement

- **SPLIT CASE PMD**
  Originator: Unknown
  Tier: Solitude Fly Company
  Hook: #14-18 Daiichi 1710 or
    Tiemco 3761
  Thread: Black 8/0 UNI-Thread
  Tail: Coq de Leon fibers
  Abdomen: Nature's Spirit Fine
    Natural Dub
  Rib: Ginger Ultra Wire
  Wing: Black goose biots
  Wing Case: Yellow Razor Foam
  Legs: Coq de Leon fibers

- **BLACK BEAUTY**
  Originator: Pat Dorsey
  Tier: Duane Redford
  Hook: #18-22 Tiemco 2487, 2488,
    or 101
  Thread: Black 8/0 UNI-Thread
  Abdomen: 8/0 UNI-Thread,
    wrapped
  Rib: Gold Ultra Wire, reverse wrapped
  Thorax: Black beaver, rabbit fur, or
    fine dry dub

- **MAMBA MIDGE PUPA**
  Originator: Duane Redford
  Tier: Duane Redford
  Hook: #20-24 Tiemco 2487
  Thread: Black 8/0 UNI-Thread
  Abdomen: Black 8/0 UNI-Thread
  Rib: Gold Ultra Wire, reverse wrapped
  Wing: Pearl Flashabou
  Head: Black 8/0 thread, wrapped,
    with head cement

- **SOUTH PLATTE SHIM**
  Originator: Tom Uba
  Tier: Tom Uba
  Hook: #20-22 Tiemco 2488
  Thread: Black 70-denier Ultra
    Thread
  Abdomen: Black 70-denier Ultra
    Thread and Rio UV Knot Sealer
  Rib: Blue Sulky Metallic Thread
  Wing: Johnson & Johnson unwaxed
    dental floss
  Head: Black Superfine Dry-Fly
    Hareline Dubbin

- **GRAPHIC CADDIS**
  Originator: John Barr
  Tier: Duane Redford
  Hook: #14-18 Tiemco 2499SPBL
  Thread: Brown 8/0 UNI-Thread (for
    thorax) and white 8/0 UNI-Thread
    (for abdomen)
  Abdomen: Silver Holographic
    Flashabou
  Legs: Tan or olive microtubing
  Head: Natural gray ostrich herl

- **MERCER'S BEADHEAD GOLDEN
  BIOT EPOXY STONEFLY**
  Originator: Mike Mercer
  Tier: Duane Redford
  Hook: #8-18 Tiemco 2302
  Bead: Gold tungsten
  Thread: Wood duck 70-denier Ultra
    Thread
  Tail: Sulphur orange turkey biots
  Rib: Gold Ultra Wire, reverse wrapped
  Wing Case: Mottled turkey tail quill
    under 5 Minute Epoxy
  Thorax: Mercer's Buggy Nymph
    Dubbing (Golden Stone)
  Legs: Mottled brown hen